"What a truly gifted and inspiring young writer! I found this book so enlightening, it encompasses many teachings and philosophies of life that can guide you towards a more meaningful and wholesome way of living. Everyone needs to read this book at least once!" – M.D.P, France

"From the very moment I started reading I felt I could relate to everything that was written. It has truly touched my heart and made me feel comforted in very difficult moments of my life that I have recently experienced. I could not control my tears in many parts of the book as I felt the messages were so personal to me. I could not recommend a better book to anyone who is seeking to change their life. This is a story of how enlightenment can truly change someone's life for the better and why we should not conform to society's norms but we should follow our hearts and do what we truly believe in." – V.L, Poland

"… This book gave me peace and, especially, it gave me hope and strength to keep digging and re-searching for my inner self, for my Soul." – A.A, Italy

"Beautiful, interesting & revealing. Personally I find *Twenty8* to be an open door to another dimension of how to become the best version of one self. A life trip of steady realisation and constant investigation which ends with a "one way enlightening path". I highly recommend this read to anybody who is looking to put some light into their life and doesn't know how or where to start. Here you have a real example to follow." – M.G, Spain

"I found this book to be quite inspiring and it makes me want to make changes for the better. This will not only be beneficial for me but also for my beautiful children." – A.F, Australia

Twenty8

The Age of Power

Fabienne Sandoval

Published by Gold Key Publications Ltd.

ISBN 978-1-5272-1660-0

For information write to Gold Key Publications:
info@goldkeypublications.com

Cover art and design by Jason Anscomb.

Edited by Suzie Grogan.

For You.

For those that are lost.
For the truth seekers.
For the wanderers.
For the magical ones.
For those seeking purpose.

To the Reader

This is a true account of the events that occurred in my life at the age of twenty-eight. There could be events or situations, presenting themselves in the book as if it were a mystical novel, but this is a tale of truth. These events did manifest themselves, in the same way this book has manifested itself into your hands.
I am grateful to share my truth with you, which I hope inspires and enchants you.

My gift to each reader is that their personal power will be resurrected as they read my story so that they too will be able to unveil the truth and live in harmony with their soul.

I have used the end of each chapter to summarise my thoughts of the journeys I experienced. I am not declaring myself as a master in these fields by any means. This is purely an opportunity for me to share with you the lessons I have learned. Please take from this what resonates with you and leave the rest.

Table of Contents

Introduction

For as long as I can remember, my mum had a fascination with the age twenty-eight.

To me, age was nothing but a number.

To her, this was the age of power.

In her own personal experience, she had encountered a dramatic shift during her twenty-eighth year. As she describes it, it was the year she became her *true* self. I spent many years hearing the magical stories that graced my mum's age of power, curiously awaiting this birthday.

Once I became twenty-eight a whole new world unfolded. It is here that my story begins, one week before my birthday. As we journey through my treacherous heartbreak, my awakening through veganism, my wanderlust, healing and quest to find the truth, you may find that this book inspires you to make changes in your own life.

My journey of awakening commenced after I transitioned to a vegan lifestyle, and I truly believe that veganism sparked the expansion of my consciousness. I also met an extraordinary gentleman, who became my teacher. He guides me towards the truth and I embark on a whole new phase. This is how my introduction to metaphysics begins. As the story unfolds you will be surprised at the stories you may read.

I soon found my own fascination with the age of twenty-eight, and realised my mother had been right all along. As the year unravelled I became convinced that twenty-eight was a special age, but as I delved into the world of metaphysics and I came to learn about astrology, I understood this to be the effects of the Saturn Return, which occurs every 28-30 years. My mother's philosophy was correct; she just had not related it back to the stars. Twenty-eight was special for her, and it would be forever special to me too.

After understanding this, I began to realise that many great thinkers had already realised the significance of the number twenty-eight. For example, in Hebrew Gematria, 'koakh' means "power" or "energy" and is a word that corresponds to the number 28. There seemed to be more to numbers than met my humble eyes – they are not just numbers, they hold great meaning. Interestingly, I found that the word 'progression' added up to the number twenty-eight, using the Pythagorean system of numerology.

- Awake in English Reduction = 28 (1+5+1+2+5)
- Evolves in English Reduction = 28 (5+4+6+3+4+5+1)
- Grows in English Reduction = 28 (7+9+6+5+1)

Before my twenty-eighth year, I was living a normal life. I enjoyed travel, shopping, make-up; the things usual for a twenty-something girl. I had a career in the corporate world that most would dream of. My aspirations were high and I was determined to reach them. My upbringing had been fairly normal, and although I was raised with a religious faith, it was only until I was ten so I didn't feel it made an impact. I wasn't exposed to anything strange or uncommon, or even remotely spiritual. I come from a loving family, despite it being a 'broken' home – my mum loved us with all her might and although I missed having a dad around, I was taken care of. I had nothing to complain about, as far as life stories go. Apart from dealing with my dad's disappearance, which did hurt me more deeply than I would like to admit, and it seemed to find its way into my romantic relationships and cause me even more pain than necessary.

In simple terms, my journey through twenty-eight led me to become a 'hippy'... well, at least this is how my friends have described my transition. If hippy means happy, then I am quite pleased with that tag. True happiness seems rare these days, so I guess it's the easiest way for them to label me. Although as you will read, I am not a fan of labels. They constrain us.

Be my guest and unveil the truth behind my twenty-eighth year, page by page. This is my tale of veganism, metaphysics and the reclamation of personal power.

Part I

This breakdown was my intuition speaking loud and clear.

1

Twenty8

I sat there a lifeless, soulless creature. The sparkle in my eyes was diminished. I was a fraction of my former self.

Broken.

Damaged from the emotional torture I had endured.

Where had I gone wrong? Well, I had not listened to my intuition. I had allowed logic to run the show. *As always.*

My heart was in tatters from the pain that remained since my daddy left all those years back. I wasn't craving romance. I was searching for a prop; a man to love me and fill his void. This was my first mistake in love and the start of the spiral of events that shaped my life so dramatically throughout this year.

::

I wrestled with my inner emotions but we were a month away from our move-in date.

Lex loved me.

We were happy.

Our life wasn't particularly exciting but it worked for me, for now.

When I met him I had just started to become curious about our human evolution – who I was and why I was here. But my progress was hindered, as I allowed my heart to become overrun with emotions and the idea of happily ever after.

Lex presented me with a very important lesson in love, one I had been trying to learn for years, yet failing at disastrously. The Universe was determined to make sure I learned the meaning of this once and for all.

We began our relationship in the spring and I was convinced it would be more than just a summer romance. On our first date, he seemed so interested in who I was, telling me "I want to know everything about you". It was the perfect meet-cute.

I fell in love with him so very quickly. It was impossible not to. He was everything I ever wished for. He took care of me and would go out of his way to make sure I was safe. He was my comforter and my protector. For the first time, I felt as though I finally had picked a good guy. He wasn't overly attractive and only earned a basic wage but I loved him for all of his other qualities. I loved him because of how much he loved me.

We were so in love then. We barely spent a moment apart, our passion and love too fierce for either one of us to deny. We used to spend our Sunday's walking along the river, in the same way we had on our first date. He would tell me: "this is just the beginning of our journey" and I believed him.

In the heat of our lust, he asked me to start a life with him and I agreed. He promised me a future and I was flattered at the idea of becoming his wife and the mother to his children.

::

I had never truly understood my worth. This was something I struggled with desperately and led me down the wrong path when it came to entering romantic relationships. My daddy left when I was a mere fourteen, just at the age when a girl really needs her father to protect her from all those silly boys who are bound to break her heart. Mine had vanished into thin air. It was as if he never existed.

But I knew he was real, I felt the loss of his love every single day. It was an unbearable pain. I couldn't broach the subject without welling up. The loss of a father is something I do not wish upon anyone. This experience would shape certain parts of my being, preparing me for the future. I learned strength and resilience through this negative situation.

Sadly though, I lost the ability to trust in men, and I was forever repeating the harsh circle of pain by allowing myself to enter relationships that would end up in the same way – I would feel abandoned, or even worse, I wouldn't allow myself the possibility of being hurt and I would run as soon as the going got tough.

This pain of the loss of my father surfaced in every romantic relationship I entered into. I didn't realise until later down the line that at every breakup I was actually mourning the death of the relationship with my father.

::

The story begins about a week before my twenty-eighth birthday. I had an unexpected breakdown and was crying uncontrollably. This was my intuition speaking loud and clear, but I didn't want to listen. The mental struggle that played out left my inner voice silenced. I blocked it out – I know better, I am right, I thought. So headstrong. So closed. Oh, how wrong I was about to be.

Our intuition speaks loudly to us for a purpose, it is our instinctive protection. As I travelled along my journey I have learned to trust it. Sometimes it is impossible for us to know why we feel a certain way but we must listen. This message is coming from a higher source. If we choose to override it we can guarantee we will be wrong.

I couldn't be honest with myself about the reasons for my breakdown. But I was freaking out about the upcoming move with Lex. It was my mum that uncovered the reasons behind my collapse: "it's the move, you have doubts" she told me. She was

19

right, my relationship anxiety surfaced but I tried to ignore my internal fears that Lex was going to abandon me just like my daddy did all those years ago. I had been hiding from the cracks in our relationship. His tendency to hold onto me so tightly left me gasping for air, and made me hold on tightly too, which was not a healthy way to maintain a relationship.

In a relationship, you always hope the pros outweigh the cons. For us, this was not the case. We had been just fine until I began to see his true colours and felt unable to accept them. I was wearing rose-tinted glasses, but deep down I was questioning the longevity of our relationship.

I told Lex that it was too soon and I could do with more time, especially since we hadn't even found a place to live. We agreed to postpone our move by a month. I felt better knowing I had salvaged some more time in my current life, but my anxiety multiplied. I was not myself and even though I knew I felt bad, I was unable to connect with myself and speak the truth - the one thing I needed more than anything.

Our feelings whether positive or negative, are a sign. They guide us to know what is really going on. They shine the light on situations even if we are not ready to be honest with ourselves. These negative feelings I was experiencing: anxiety, depression, and the feeling of being overwhelmed, were telling me that something was wrong with my life. Unfortunately, it took me a little while to really understand them.

::

I had everything society told me I should desire and more. Little did I know that this wasn't enough. This breakdown was the beginning of my breakthrough and my journey of ascension.

Even though I was feeling an array of emotions, I pushed forward with my plans. Lex and I spent every Saturday scrutinising properties in the suburbs. This made me feel like a grown-up, heading in the right direction. At almost thirty, this is what I wanted - at least that's what I thought. I wanted to settle down, live in the country and have a family – the usual flow of life and the one accepted by most individuals and enforced upon us by society.

::

About a month after my first freak-out, where my anxious nature had got the better of me and I was left unsettled, tears streaming, the second warning sign appeared. As I sat across the table from him, I knew something was wrong. The property we had just viewed was perfect for us. It met all of the requirements but there was something in his eyes that showed resistance. As we discussed our needs and how the property matched up, I felt the knot in my stomach tighten. He was harsh and reserved and I felt as though he was having second thoughts.

It had been my birthday a couple of weeks before, and he had met my family for the first time. It did not go well. It was important to me that he made a good impression as I was extremely close to my family, but he failed that test. We did not walk away with my mum's seal of approval and I so desperately needed that. In fact, I wasn't impressed with him either. For the first time in eight months he had not lived up to my expectations. It was as if he didn't care what my family thought of him. This confused and saddened me. We fought about it, of course, but he dismissed it saying that he was having a bad day. I wanted to believe him so I let it go. My family, on the other hand, were not so forgiving, and rightfully so.

As we sat face to face at the table in this perfectly calm restaurant, he was unable to communicate with me so I broke down crying. In an attempt to regain control I felt him forcefully withdrawing. My inner child became scared of being abandoned - maybe he didn't love me anymore?

I left to compose myself in the ladies bathroom. I should have walked away there and then, but something drove me to stay. When I returned we continued to attempt communication but it did not go well.

We left the restaurant with a vulnerability in our relationship that had only just surfaced. As we drove back to his place, in silence for the entire journey, I contemplated leaving and spending the night at my own place. I told him of my intention but he wouldn't let me. His loving side returned and he begged me not to go. The deep inner need I had to be loved took over and I gave in to him, instead of following my gut instinct.

The following week, we lost out on that property and our move was up in the air, but this was the least of my worries, as the relationship itself now seemed to be uncertain. He wasn't loving or excited about our future anymore. The very person who had instigated this major life change was distant and afraid. However, after we had both discussed our fears and our past relationship ghosts we agreed it was the right next step and continued with our move.

We were both entitled to cold feet, right?

::

I was about to leave for a three-week adventure. I believed some time apart would be good for us. Absence makes the heart grow fonder they say...

Absence surely did make the heart grow fonder for Lex and I, and the thought of being alone was too much for either of us to bear. Every day I was gone we longed to be back in each other's warm, familiar arms.

Instead of facing the inevitable we continued forth with the move. We found a delightful house in the suburbs and in our fear of a lonesome singleton future we made an offer to the estate agent. Our offer was accepted and we were excited once again, visualising our perfect, happy life together in our new home.

In the cold, dark winter we moved to the countryside. After months of searching, we had found a place to call home - the most charming house with creaks in all the right places and a living room the size of a pea. Despite our quaint cottage, I was still riddled with uncertainty.

As I packed up my old life and the last of the boxes were put inside the van I felt sad. Sad to be leaving my home behind along with all the happy memories and the tranquillity I had created with my sister. These would now be consigned to the past. This was normal, I reassured myself. We have to let go of the old to make way for the new.

However, we did not get off to a good start from day one, and if I am completely honest our relationship wasn't the same after my sudden turn a couple of months before. I desperately tried to repair the damage, but it was too late. He too was changing. I didn't know what was different but I couldn't seem to be with him in the way I was before. It felt as though he was withholding his love from me, and unable to express it to me in the way he had done before.

Maybe we were no longer energetically tied and maybe our paths were not moving in the same direction. Although this was true, I was unable to understand it at the time.

Over the course of the next three weeks, our relationship deteriorated day by day. I could not ignore the signs that I was receiving - something was wrong. The person I believed I was moving in with was someone else altogether and not at all who he had been while we dated. As the days passed by I became more and more afraid of the monster I was living with.

I had a constant knot in my stomach.

Home is a place of comfort and peace but I found myself on the battlefield, unprepared for the fight. I walked into the living room only to be reminded of my 'lesser' female position and how I was not 'entitled' to speak. I was supposed to keep quiet for the sake of the relationship. I wondered how we had reached this place. I felt as though I was going mad.

I kept replaying our conversations over and over each time my head hit the pillow and all I could do was try to find a way to fix the problems in our relationship. I tried to work out where I had driven him to become angry. I didn't like living like this and I was prepared to do anything to stop his poison-filled bullets that kept hitting me right in the middle of the chest.

Since day one of our move, it felt as if he was slowly trying to weaken me with his emotional mind games. I didn't realise it until afterwards but he was emotionally torturing me with his love; giving it and taking it away, so I would become dependent on him and I wouldn't be able to leave.

As the weeks slowly dragged by, our arguments became more intense. We had only had one fight prior to our move in but now he had so much anger inside. We were fighting almost daily. How had he hidden this side of himself so well before? During each argument he seemed intent on hurting me as much as possible, putting the blame on me each time, taking none of the responsibility.

But after yet another argument, while we were making up in the kitchen, he reached for my face to pull me close. He held my head in his hands with a tight grip. I tried to wriggle free but his eyes were serious and threatening as he said "I love you".

In that moment I became very afraid of him. This was not normal, nor was it a healthy relationship. This was about possession and control and as far as he was concerned he owned me. I played along; trying to hide my terror but I realised this was the final warning sign. My inner voice was red, loud, angry and screaming at me to get out. If I didn't listen now I feared I never would.

This relationship was killing me and I was compromising my inner being and the light I had to shine on the world. It was time I listened to the voice from within that had been trying to guide me all along.

::

The following day I fell into my mother's office in a heap. Tears were rolling down my face before I had the chance to explain anything.

"What's wrong? Why are you crying?" She said, concerned.

I could only continue to cry. I had no words. I relaxed into her embrace feeling instantly better after receiving her love. She had never really liked Lex from the start and for good reason – he pretty much ruined my birthday that year. I guess she predicted it was only a matter of time until I came to her, crying. I wept further as I talked about our deteriorating relationship. I told her how I felt he didn't love me in the same way anymore. How I had become his punch bag. How everything was my fault.

My mum spoke firmly to me: "you know what you've got to do".

My barriers came up as I resisted the information, even though I knew she was right. That day I travelled home late, knowing that this would be the end.

There's nothing lonelier than being with someone and not being seen. For the love of love, please don't ever settle. You chose how to be alone. – Simi Froman

As our fourth week in the house drew to a close, so did our relationship. It was early on the Friday evening and as much as I didn't want to, I opened up the final conversation.

I told him this was not how I expected our first month in the house to go, along with my reasons for leaving. His responses were few; he just looked at me while I spoke. He didn't like what I was saying but his pride was too fierce to admit that it wasn't what he wanted, so he agreed with me. I drove home to my family that evening and cried the rest of the night with the relief of knowing this living nightmare was soon to be over and I would be safe. Free from his clutches.

In the morning I woke up with fresh determination to move out before the end of the day. I went back to the house where I was met with hostility from a hurt man. It turned to sadness fairly quickly and a plea for us to remain friends, but I knew it wouldn't last. Packing up my shattered dreams was difficult but I knew it was the right thing to do. Two men arrived three hours later and we proceeded to move all the boxes to my very own storage unit.

I felt like I had gone from having it all, to having nothing but a storage unit. My dreams of 'happily ever after' had disappeared. I was broken; emotionally a wreck and depleted of all the previous vibrancy and energy I once embodied.

Little did I know this was only the beginning of my journey, and there was so much more to learn.

Twenty8

Teaching on Love

Love is something we all seek out. It is part of being a human. The problem is, we are so scared of being alone that we make stupid mistakes in order to fool ourselves into living the romantic dream. The world fools us with romantic fantasies that are not at all true. Love is not about uttering those three special words. Love is about *being*.

Love is all we are.

The great Indian spiritual leader, Osho, shared the following analogy about love, which expresses perfectly the lessons I have learned and my current beliefs.

The capacity to be alone is the capacity to love. It may look paradoxical to you, but it's not. It is an existential truth: only those people who are capable of being alone are capable of love, of sharing, of going into the deepest core of another person--without possessing the other, without becoming dependent on the other, without reducing the other to a thing, and without becoming addicted to the other. They allow the other absolute freedom, because they know that if the other leaves, they will be as happy as they are now. Their happiness cannot be taken by the other, because it is not given by the other. – Osho

Let us enjoy the presence of love without the urge to hold onto it and without the desire to pluck it like a flower. To love is to let the other person be who they are, with no conditions - to let them run free. For now, I see myself as a wildflower. I don't want to be spoiled or tamed, I want to be able to grow to my fullest capacity and I want to love and be loved in this way.

We will never evolve and participate in a beautiful lasting soul connection with another until we stop entering relationships based on 'need'. I used to be someone that evaluated love based on a 'list' of all the qualities my future partner would have.

For example, he would be in a good job, have a nice car, money etc. This kind of thinking is so far from the truth and essence of what love is it is no wonder I had not been successful.

Love in its truest form is not a transaction. The Sun does not say "you were miserable yesterday so today I will not shine". Love is eternal and nature shows us the way with endless giving, which is true love.

Embody love and give love always - in every action, in every word, in every touch and only then will you find the true meaning of love, and how it has always been within you. The lack of love is the lack of consciousness and eternal peace.

And just as the flowers bloomed in the spring, new buds finally blossoming upon the bare branches, the chains that had their firm grip around her fell away and she was able to be herself once more.

2

Cutting the Cord

I had only just begun unveiling the truth. Little did I know this first battle would not be the last in this amazing year. Nonetheless, it was all directional and required by the Universe to place me where I needed to be. Starting over isn't always something we welcome with open arms, but sometimes it is necessary to push us into the new life we are supposed to live. For this, we must be grateful to the Universe and its wondrous powers, even if that makes no sense to us at the time. It is important that we trust the process.

While I was nursing my heart back to into shape and tending to the bruises, my mind began to sway towards the idea that this had all occurred for a good reason.

Life can only be understood backwards, but it must be lived forwards. – Soren Kierkegaard

I was feeling hopeful about my future and the purpose behind all these dramatic events.

But Lex just wouldn't let me go.

Oh why, oh why did he have to hold on so?

Unfortunately, Lex was not so thrilled about the idea of starting over and he continued to seek me out. He was unable to let me move on with my life and every time I left the house I would have to consider the likelihood of him following me. I was constantly on my guard and it was unsettling, to say the least. I frequently bumped into him and was always met with the same hurt and pain-ridden man as the day I moved out. It was emotionally exhausting.

For anyone that has experienced heartbreak, I am sure you will appreciate that the first weeks are the worst. The death of a relationship can be hard to withstand because we are still carrying their energy with us and part of our being is still held with another soul. Eventually, we reclaim those parts of ourselves back; but it takes time.

Time was of the essence though. I was unable to continue in this way and I longed to find a way to separate myself from him.

One day, whilst mid-thought on this very subject, I looked up to see a gentleman standing there right in front of me. I had been so distracted that I hadn't even recognised him. He looked familiar but I couldn't place him.

I then remembered that this gentleman had been around for some time. He was only an acquaintance, but he seemed to keep popping up, offering advice as if by magic. His timing was impeccable and always right when I needed it.

It was as if he had heard my thoughts that day, as he began to offer me some of his usual type of advice, even though I did not recall ever telling him about my problems. His solutions were different from those of the average person. He seemed to know a lot about metaphysics, a subject I had no desire to learn about or understand. In truth, I wasn't really sure what 'metaphysics' meant, and I thought it best not to pay too much attention to him.

However, I was extremely curious to find out what he had to say and was a little nervous in his presence. He was different, to say the least, but I didn't have the time to think about why or how. I was desperate for Lex to leave me in peace and it seemed like this 'Magical Metaphysical Man' had the answer to my problem. Despite being nervous, something deep inside told me to trust him, so I did, implicitly. He suggested a cutting of the cords exercise[1] to assist in breaking the energetic connection between Lex and I.

I performed the exercise later that evening and immediately felt its effects. I noticed how much freer and lighter I felt from Lex as his energy left me. I was able to breathe again, and I could slowly begin to feel parts of myself that had been lost for so long. As they returned, so did my passion and zest for life; the dark clouds were clearing and I trusted that this pain I was experiencing was part of the greater good to come.

This Magical Metaphysical Man was right; maybe metaphysics was not so scary after all. He seemed to possess all the knowledge of the Universe, and so I contemplated what else I may be able to learn from him. But how would I contact him? He didn't even own a mobile phone...

::

I'll admit being at home with my family was very comforting initially, but after a few weeks of living out of boxes and sharing a room with my sister, I decided that, in order to truly heal, I needed to have my space. The time had come to brave the world as a grown-up again. I had to move forward onto the unknown path that had been carved out for me.

I believe our home plays a huge part of creating a peaceful life; it is one of the foundations of living a beautiful, content and happy existence.

After manifesting the exact home I had dreamt of for years, I had to go through the same process I had been through twice in the last two months. More removal vans, boxes, packing and unpacking! I was exhausted by moving.

As I returned to the storage unit and to all my possessions, I was reminded of the unhappy circumstances last

---

[1] This exercise is given at the end of the chapter.

time I had been there. I struggled to hold myself together, overcome by my emotions. I was grateful to start again but it was tough living in a new home, adapting to a new life I hadn't planned for.

Teaching on Cutting the Cord

I used this exercise to remove the energetic connection between myself and Lex. I have since used this for other relationships where I wish to disconnect, and it does not just have to be used in the romantic sense. I believe this to be a very powerful exercise and I experienced almost instantaneous results. Complete this exercise when you have a moment of peace, alone and with no distractions.

You will need:
- 1 small bowl of salt water
- Tea Tree Oil
- Bath Salts

1. Imagine a number of white etheric energy cords emanating from your solar plexus. Visualise these cords connecting you to the person in question.

2. In one hand, take hold of all the cords at the front of the chest where they attach to the solar plexus; with the other hand imagine white light shining out of the tips of each of your fingers as 'blades'. Begin to make chopping motions – cutting off the cords with the 'blades' of white light.

3. Take the chopped off ends of the cords – those that are still attached to the person in question and are now disconnected from you – and put them into a bowl of concentrated salt water. It is preferable to use unrefined sea salt as detailed below.

4. Take a 20-30 minute salt and tea tree bath. Fill the bath with ½-1 kg of unrefined, Sun-dried Celtic sea salt. Add 12 drops of Tea Tree or Lavender essential oil.
   Note: These baths can be taken several times per week (or, if necessary, daily) and serve to clear negative, "dirty" energy from the chakras and personal bio-field. As a consequence, they have a healing, revitalising effect whilst calming, stabilising and uplifting the emotions.

5. Relax in the knowing that the detachment is complete.

The process had begun, she was awakening. First, we had to remove the negative drains on her; secondly, we had to stir her from her slumber. It was a slow process but once she was awakened then she would truly be living and able to enter the age of power.

3

An Awakening

I had spent most of my life accepting the way the world was and bowing down to society's rules, ever the obedient follower, until I was hurled into my awakening. When was the last time you questioned why you do the things you do?

I had been a carnivore my whole life, never questioning my food habits or the cultural norm. I was just getting to grips with all the new parts of my life, when somebody dropped the V bomb! A family friend, who was considering becoming vegan[2], had shared a video from YouTube with my sister. My sister watched and immediately shared it with me – posing a challenging question: "Do you want to be vegan?" Upon reading her message I knew this video must include information that was about to change my life forever.

It was KatyHemFit's video entitled *Why I've Become Vegan*. After watching the video I knew I had to understand veganism at a deeper level, but I instantly resonated with the information. In my heart, it was the right thing to do. This video exposed many things that were unknown to me.

---

[2] A vegan does not consume meat, dairy products, eggs, honey, or any product derived from an animal.

I recognised the damage consuming animal products did to the animals, but I was shocked to find out the effect it has on our planet and the negative impact on our health.

I couldn't stand by knowing that world hunger could be eliminated through moving to a vegan diet.

My first thoughts were that it was going to be difficult and restrictive, but I was surprised at how easy I found it. After reviewing the meals I had eaten that day, I realised that two out of the three meals were vegan anyway.

To go vegan overnight was quite a big jump and not one that many people make, but once I had decided this lifestyle made sense to me, I saw no reason to complete the transition gradually. One day I was eating meat, the next I had cleared out my kitchen and was staring into the bare cupboards trying to decide what to make for dinner.

I began to watch a number of documentaries – *Knives over Forks* and *Cowspiracy*, along with speeches by activists such as Gary Yourofsky[3], James Aspey[4] and YouTube videos by the Life Regenerator and Raw Alignment. I wanted to arm myself with knowledge and understand why I was opting for this kind of lifestyle. These activists and speakers truly inspired me to jump headfirst into this exciting new phase of my life.

Sometimes in our heart, we immediately know what to do but with a topic as controversial as veganism I wanted to be able to answer the difficult questions about why I was going to be living a life different to the norm. I also wanted to know what it was that made me change my mind overnight and figure out what it was that made me feel the way I did.

Was I doing it for the animals? Or for my health? Was it a moral decision? There were many questions I wanted to uncover.

---

[3] The Most Important Speech You Will Ever Hear by Gary Yourofsky.

[4] This Speech Is Your WAKE UP CALL! by James Aspey.

Harm to our Animals

Despite never being an animal lover, the pain I felt most and one of the reasons that led me to empathise with the vegan lifestyle was, in fact, the harm we inflict on animals. Especially as a woman, it was difficult to accept how we treat cows.

I was horrified to learn that many face a tragic cycle. Firstly, they are artificially inseminated. They are pregnant for almost the same amount of time as humans – on average 283 days; and then after giving birth to their precious newborn they are painfully separated, within moments. The cows and calves scream in agony and the milk that should be used to feed the newborn is stolen for humans to enjoy. If this process was conducted on you or me, we would all be in an uproar, but since it's an animal with no voice we seem to ignore the true hard facts.

Is milk really so delicious that it's worth us treating other beings in this way?

I discovered that cow's milk can **legally** contain up to 400 million pus cells per litre. So one teaspoonful of milk can have two million pus cells![5] I was disgusted and horrified. I had always known that eating meat would entail the death of an animal so this information was really not surprising, but watching the footage in documentaries was heart-breaking.

I quickly realised that these acts were not in alignment with my beliefs. If you value life, then does it really matter which being's life it is? I do not condone war so why would I support the mass murder that occurs in the farming industry day after day?

I feel we should all be treated with the same respect. I decided that I did not want to contribute to the death of another being, whether I was the one doing the slaughtering or not.

---

[5] whitelies.org.uk

Harm to our Planet

The next thing that shocked me was the disturbing impact of factory farming on our planet. Yet despite all of the environmental warnings, we are never publicly advised that veganism is the solution. Why?

Because we live in a consumerist world where making money stands for more than caring for our planet.

The United Nations has stated that animal agriculture is the largest contributor to greenhouse gases - larger than all forms of transport. This means in order to make a positive environmental impact on the world, instead of selling our cars and using bicycles we would actually make a greater impact by reducing the amount of meat we eat.

Worldhunger.org states that 700 million tonnes of human-grade food goes into animal agriculture each year. This is food that could be used to eradicate hunger.

How is it possible that many in the western world have everything, yet there are others still dying of hunger every day?

Harm to our Health

Despite the wealth of information I had, the first month of being vegan didn't come without its challenges. The first issue I faced was how to nourish myself. During the first four weeks, I became very bloated and rarely felt hungry which I now understand to be my detox period. My body was not used to so many beautiful life foods and it was clearing my system out, removing all of the negative substances that had been infecting my body for years.

Every staple, go-to meal I had eaten previously had now become off limits and meal time became a carefully thought out process. It took a little while to adjust. Like all change, initially it is scary and unknown, but then it becomes normal.

I found there was a whole range of foods that could provide me with the required nutrients. I began to incorporate beans, legumes, grains, nuts and seeds, but my primary diet consisted of fruits and vegetables. I found freedom and no longer felt restricted. I could eat as much as I liked of these beautiful life foods which replenished me with the vitamins and minerals I had been missing in my previous diet, whilst infusing my body with an abundance of life force.

There are so many resources online to help with the transition; it doesn't need to be difficult. David Jubb's books, *Secrets of an Alkaline Body* and *LifeFood Recipe Book: Living on Life Force* were extremely helpful during this period and woke me up to further information about many technical and esoteric aspects of nutrition.

After the initial adjustment and detoxification process was complete, my energy levels went through the roof. I was waking up before my alarm, bursting with energy, feeling vibrant and alive for the first time in months.

The peace and lightness I gained were indescribable. The heavy negative energy that surrounded the dead flesh I had previously consumed was no longer draining my body of its natural resources. For most of us, this only becomes apparent – and forcefully so – when we ingest raw, living foods in the forms in which nature has produced them and through experiencing the dramatic elevation of mind, body and spirit which occurs.

::

Culturally, we are so set in our ways we rarely question why we do things the way we do. This is something that has changed dramatically for me. I am constantly asking the question, why? Why do we do that? Why do I do that? Is it because I have been so programmed by a culture that simply believes this is normal? Or is it because that is what is in my heart and I really want to do it?

Many of us are leading a life created by society's ideas of what we *should* do.

Unfortunately, we are not as free as we believe we are and therefore we must practice and cultivate freedom. We must learn to become truth seekers and not rely on global leaders to provide us with relevant, accurate information. We expect to be told if something is bad for us. Sadly the world is not set up this way. It's all about what makes money. After watching *What the Health* I understood the way that the world is structured. Our charities are sponsored by companies that are part of the problem. The industrial agri-businesses, pharmaceutical companies and the government are all in bed with one another. It is depressing, to say the least. But we must take the responsibility to educate ourselves and understand what is truly going on. Only then can we make an informed choice and know which is the best path to take.

We have to vote with our pound, for this is the best way to bring about change. The supply is only there because we demand it. If our demand is for organic, nutrient-dense, produce then we will drive out the foods that are damaging to our health and the planet.

I found that my spiritual evolution happened quickly after I had become vegan. It was unbearable knowing that I had not been correctly informed about the damaging effects of animal agriculture. I soon learned how much danger our planet and our health are in. You only have to Google 'Plastic Island', 'SLS', 'Monsanto', 'HAARP', 'ChemTrails' or 'Cobalt Mining' and you will find a whole host of other violations to sift through.

We need to be more aware than ever in order to protect our planet and our health. As a result of veganism I became wildly curious about the rest of the world and the secrets I had yet to discover. I was finally awake. My consciousness had been set free from all of the lies I had been consuming on a daily basis. There was a fire raging inside me that could not be stopped.

I wanted the truth.

Teaching on Compassion

Compassion is a powerfully positive emotion. When you tap into this, your life will expand in a million ways. You will feel pure and connected on a deeper level, deeper than you ever have done before. This is not a lesson on veganism but on compassion. We can all do with showing more awareness and consideration as to what is happening around us.

See the individual in the office with no friends, the person crying on the tube platform, the pregnant lady on the bus? Take time to look outside yourself and see where you can be compassionate towards others. It will change your life in the most positive of ways.

For me, the gift of veganism allowed me to open up my heart and my life to a more compassionate way of living. It was the start of something beautiful and a path that I feel truly honours the planet and all its life forms.

I experienced a direct correlation between my diet and my consciousness. As soon as I began to eat a plant-based diet high in fresh fruit and vegetables, my consciousness began to expand. I have seen the same effects on countless friends who were inspired by my change. Even the greats knew this - Pythagoras, Buddha, Plato, Socrates, and Einstein are all said to have been vegetarians.

The truth was unveiling itself because she had asked it to do so. The Universe heard her request and proceeded to take over, showing her the way. There were storms ahead, demons to abolish and other areas of growth for her to undertake. This would require breaking her heart once again in the process. A little rain never hurt anyone, and only enabled the flowers to flourish.

4

Corporate Robot

The next aspect of my life to change was my much-loved career. I had worked incredibly hard to achieve a set of goals that were carefully calculated by me, aged sixteen. I had strategically planned for months how I would get to the final point on my list - the one that would make me feel I had 'made it'. Oh, how superficial of me. I was still growing and there was much to be discovered.

My professional calling started with a dream to work at a specific corporate conglomerate, travel the world and work my way up the ladder. I was only young but was convinced that this was what I was going to do. I wrote to the company multiple times over my summer break and ended up getting an interview, but by this point, I'd already been offered a position with another company. At the end of my interview with my chosen firm, when asked if I had any questions, I asked when I would find out if I was successful. I told them of my situation and my vision of working there. The woman interviewing me disappeared for a few moments and returned with a smile on her face, "You've got the job!" she declared. I was ecstatic; it seemed my dreams were coming true.

So I began working at sweet sixteen, bypassing the education system and cutting straight to the chase. After university, a job with prospects was the goal anyway, so why wait all those years? I was determined to make something of myself - without the degree.

I always despised school and when given the opportunity to leave I closed the door and never looked back. A formal education is not everything. Why? Because the wise will teach themselves. Nothing I have come to learn and understand was ever taught to me at school. It was all through my own personal studies.

::

As I had begun to move forward in the light I was struck by more darkness. For the previous six months, my long-awaited promotion had been within my reach, until the management changed during the hiring process. Throughout my career I had met some challenging individuals, most of them toughening me up, preparing me for the next step in my career, but no one was like this manager-to-be.

I learned early on that niceties did not get you ahead, nor were they found in this type of environment. In an attempt to remain myself, I kept my morals but created a strict set of rules in order to adhere to the corporate robotic standards. One of these was the unwritten rule that there should be no crying, under any circumstances. I wished to keep a hold of my true self but some human characteristics had to go if I wanted to succeed.

They told me: 'climb the ladder, chase success, status and money – this buys you happiness'.

It is sad to say that like most of us I had not established, nor understood, the concept of a balanced life and I spent most of my time working for non-existent brownie points, all in my mistaken attempt to get ahead and live the life of my dreams. A true corporate robot indeed.

::

At this point in my life, my career meant everything to me and the hard work I had poured into my job over the last three years was about to pay off and the promotion I so desperately wanted would be mine. Or so I thought.

That's when I met *her*. From the outset, I immediately noticed her blackened energy and condescending tone. Never in my life have I seen another human being interact with others in such a careless, unkind manner. The constant put-downs and lack of trust were disappointing and tiring. Some people, it seems, won't be happy until they've pushed others into the ground.

Unfortunately, as fate would have it she was about to be my new boss. I kept my cool despite the fact that I was feeling the burden of this negative, compassionless woman. It was almost as if she was without feelings, but I could tell it was all to support the inner mean girl that was ruling every aspect of her life. I felt nothing but sorrow for her. Out of her own desperation to feel important and in control, she happily trod on others around her.

Sadly, many corporations perpetuate this negative behaviour. I do not blame her. We are all a product of our environment and it was a shame to think she had been taken by the storm we can easily get lost in. They do not refer to this as 'selling your soul to the devil' for nothing. Yes, you get the security and the money, but is that what truly matters?

I wasn't the only one experiencing these personal issues with her. When you're fondly thought of by others you are bound to encounter some who dislike you. It wasn't as if I expected everyone to always like me. But to have another human being go out of their way to make my life hell was not something I thought I would encounter in a professional environment. This is what I had read in newspapers, books and had seen in TV dramas. I didn't realise that bullying in the workplace was a real issue; I thought we left that behind in secondary school, where it belonged. Miserably though, 8 out of 10 workers are affected by workplace bullying at some time or another.

::

I think my biggest disappointment was that I actually had faith that, if this day ever came, I would be supported by my company. How wrong I was. After being fed all of the usual corporate 'bullshit' about values and morals, I quickly realised those things don't exist when you are in this situation. It seems almost impossible to *prove* that you are being bullied, especially if you wish to remain professional, mature and dignified.

In the beginning, I chose the mature route and attempted an honest, open conversation to establish a working relationship and discuss the issues that I was facing with *her*, but she did not listen to me. It was *her* way or the high way. I have never felt so alone in a place I used to call home.

After the treacherous time I had endured with Lex, I didn't think I was strong enough to go through this. I felt confined once more. I was out of options, my logical response was to resign but it was not my ideal solution. This was where my heart and soul had belonged for the last twelve years. I wasn't ready to give up on it just yet. A number of confidants suggested a resignation as the only option though.

This was until I was reconnected with an old colleague and friend. He suggested that I opt for a sabbatical, taking three months out to gain perspective and be in the position to make a solid judgement. He was right and to this day I can only thank him for his invaluable advice.

::

After two months of leaving for work in the morning filled with stress and anxiety and ending each day at home in floods of tears, I decided to walk away from my dream promotion, my current job and possibly the company. I went to my existing boss and explained very bluntly what was happening. Luckily I had not yet accepted the new position and was still able to go to him for support. I don't think he quite had any idea how badly this was affecting me.

After beginning my first sentence, however, my eyes flooded with tears and the next thing I knew I was in the middle of an emotional breakdown. I felt extremely embarrassed about it at the time, as this was, of course, against the strict rules I had so carefully carved out for myself. Now I actually question how I could feel embarrassed at crying about something that was truly causing me pain. But crying is a sign of weakness in the corporate world. Robots don't feel.

Nevertheless, the tears fell. It was difficult to stop them but I managed to say enough for him to understand and sympathise. I continued one of the most difficult conversations of my entire career by also declining the promotion. My existing boss was surprised, to say the least...

"What do you want?" he questioned.

"A sabbatical", I announced.

He gasped.

A loud "wow" shortly followed, and the next thing I knew we were arranging the details. Despite having my letter of resignation in my back pocket, I was grateful for his understanding and that I did not have to succumb to my last resort. Never had a sabbatical been agreed in this record time. It would commence in less than four weeks.

::

My main advice to anyone suffering in the workplace is: firstly, you are not alone; secondly, speak up. It was only after my ordeal and once my wounds were healed that I realised the importance of this advice. You will feel like this is your fault - and I know I blamed myself - but it is not your fault. Trust me, nobody likes a bully and if it's being done to you I am sure there is someone else close by experiencing the same treatment. In my case, there were two other women affected. It will be hard, but this will make you stronger. Speak up for yourself and anyone else that has been the victim of bullying in the workplace.

As Patricia Cori notes in *Atlantis Rising: The Struggle of Darkness and Light:*

"Remember: You can be victimised only if you believe you are powerless. You can suffer the loss of your personal power only if you believe your soul can be taken from you. And you will fear death only if you remain ignorant to the process of the soul's evolution." [6]

I had been put through the mill and it was time to step away from life as I knew it and begin the healing process. As the days passed, I couldn't count them down quickly enough.

::

As my living nightmare was coming to an end I began to reminisce upon the years gone by. I can still remember my first day...

I was wearing a Next suit that hung from me - they just didn't have suits to fit sixteen-year-old girls back then. I was in awe of the place and half scared, half excited. I had humble beginnings, starting out as a cashier in a branch. But ever the quick learner, I progressed to the next position in a matter of months.

After almost two years working in the front office, I saw a posting for a role in HQ. I immediately knew that was my next job. In those days, you used to have to ask your boss for permission to apply for roles. But when I spoke to him, he declined my request and told me I'd have to meet with the Area Director if I wanted approval.

He obviously thought I would never have the guts go to the Area Director but he underestimated me. I immediately contacted the Area Director's assistant so she could schedule a meeting for us. I was nervous walking into his office but I also had a quiet confidence. At our meeting I asked him the same question, and I was basically told I didn't have a chance. This didn't deter me. I was fiercely determined in pursuit of my dreams and no one was going to hold me back, not even the most

---

[6] Patricia Cori, *Atlantis Rising*, page 75.

senior manager I'd ever met.

He promised if I left my application with him he would sign it and have his assistant send it across. In that moment I knew we were two days away from the closing date and there was no way he was going to make sure my application arrived on time. So I took matters into my own hands and two minutes later I was calling the number on the posting and speaking to a man named Nick. I was sure he thought I was slightly crazy, but within a matter of moments I had faxed my application over.

My mother always encouraged us to believe that anything is possible, so despite being so young I never doubted myself or my ability. I had the freedom to be anything I wished to be and I believed that wholeheartedly.

I wasn't surprised when I received the call. I had an interview and I was ecstatic. I won them over with my positive energy, enthusiasm and eagerness. I got the job! I was thrilled, but my boss less so. This next role was huge for me. It was one of the most eye-opening experiences of my life. After working in the team and progressing well, a few months passed where it was just like any job, but one day I received an email.

It read: 'we will be migrating our current processes overseas and we are looking for individuals interested in travelling to India for anywhere between 1 – 6 months.'

I jumped at the chance, instantaneously responding to my boss telling her that I would love the opportunity. This was all part of my plan. Goal number two: travel the world. I was chosen to spend a month in India to migrate our processes, stretching me beyond my wildest imagination. I had gone from processor to subject matter expert overnight. My time in India is still to this very day unforgettable and life-changing. India was truly magical and I embraced every second of it.

I had never left the country alone up until this point, and I was shocked by what I found when I arrived there. I had never been so uncomfortable, this land was completely different from what I knew back home. However, this experience taught me to value my blessings, for running water and a solid roof over your head are truly a gift.

My time there taught me a lot about life and I think set the foundation for how I wanted to live it - with a permanent attitude of gratitude. I was only a mere nineteen at this point. I believe whole-heartedly that travel provides the growth of the soul and these adventures shape our reality.

Before I knew it, my time was up and I was heading home from the trip that would spark my eternal desire to travel. When you return from a trip that intense, you feel unfairly privileged to live the life you lead. I struggled to settle back into normal life, and for a good six months I tried to find an opportunity so I could move to India. In the end I took a training role-based 'on the road' in the UK. My Indian dream just wasn't meant to be, but as one of my favourite quotes states:

That which is true for you never goes away. It's always there waiting for you to show up. – Melissa Ambrosini

I knew I'd be back.
One day.
India still carries a piece of my heart.

After spending nine months on the road and exploring the majority of the UK by car, I was bored with living out of a suitcase and I craved a base that I could spend more than three or four days in. This was yet another situation where my determination saw me through to triumph. Before applying for my next role (and first managerial position) my boss told me outright I wouldn't be successful, but of course I should try for the 'experience'. I wonder what it must feel like to lose faith in your dreams and then be unable to have faith in other people's dreams too. I proceeded irrespective of the lack of confidence from my boss, and with all the power I had inside of me I visualised getting the job.

I attended the interview and when they asked, "do you think you can do this job?" my response was a powerful "yes". In that moment I knew I had the job and was called on my birthday,

54

my twenty-first birthday in fact. To this day Roger, the hiring manager, still reminds me of my enthusiasm and excitement. I accepted the role, a promotion to my first managerial grade. It was the first job where I felt I was able to spread my wings and show my full potential.

As I reminisced about my time there and the good old days when I was young, naïve and the place was in better shape, I noticed how grateful I felt for my experience there, as I had developed from a teenager to a woman. For now, it was time to look forward and after twelve years, it was time to create a new path for myself.

::

After the apparent 'mess' in my life, I was seeking a way to recover from the various setbacks, (which, in retrospect, appeared to have been "orchestrated" from above in order to shatter the status quo). Once again, I encountered the Magical Metaphysical Man, showing up out of the blue, unannounced in his typically enigmatic fashion. This divine moment with him led me to pursue more answers to my questions.

It felt as though he was there waiting in the wings, ready to appear whenever I needed him. There is an ancient saying by Tibetan Monks which states that when the student is ready, the teacher will appear. I felt so lost at this time in my life and he appeared at the perfect time to pick me up and show me the way. I had no idea I was seeking a teacher, but the teacher, sure enough, knew I was ready.

Little did I know I was about to become a student of metaphysics.

We wandered through the park, it was a beautiful day and the Sun was shining brightly. We discussed the power of the Sun and the energy it radiates.

He was so insightful, explaining how the Sun is a vital source of Prana - Prana meaning energy. Radiating its rays upon us, a fully conscious light being, it all made sense to me. I didn't know why though, this was not your average conversation.

Without the Sun, rain would be near impossible, nor would photosynthesis take place. Knowing the actions of vitamin D, it is even proven that without the Sun our happiness is at stake.

Despite knowing that the Sun must be important to us, I had rarely ever stopped to consider its benefits. My mind was always consumed by other thoughts that seemed to hold more importance. The simplicity yet depth of our conversation was so appealing.

::

He guided me through an exercise where I drew higher dimensional frequencies from the Sun. This exercise felt very natural to me and only took a few moments to complete. Afterwards, I was in a meditative state, unsure what this exercise achieved but knowing I felt very good following it. My thoughts then trailed off...

He was the most magical, interesting, knowledgeable person I had ever met. Still, I barely knew a thing about him, despite our meetings becoming more frequent, we always seemed to run out of time. He was very mysterious.

The following days after I had drawn in the frequencies from the Sun, I found many positive manifestations came into my life. It was not through chance - I was sure there was something in this strange, yet simple, exercise. It seemed to raise my consciousness and potential, enabling me to operate on a higher frequency than before.

I had never been exposed to this kind of cosmic teaching before, so it was not surprising that I was cautious - a little scared and unsure what to expect. He had promised me the teachings would enhance my life, but who was I to trust this stranger who had entered my life without any introduction?

I didn't want to be gullible and I was very aware that my naivety about the subject could land me in some kind of trouble.

It was this solar technique that drew me closer to him, wanting more knowledge, information and exercises. Even though I spent many an hour in confusion. Yes, I wanted to know more, but I did not really know what I was doing there.

This subject was way out of my comfort zone and I disliked the lack of control I had over the situation. I constantly questioned myself if it was the right choice to be listening to his teachings, but since I had a sense of peace and belonging with him I found myself happily agreeing to his strange techniques. It was as if I was just relearning something I already knew to be the truth. I felt that he had been placed in my life for some reason and I must follow its course through.

Teaching on Expectations

From the moment we are born we are introduced to a life full of expectations - our parent's expectations of who they want us to be when we grow up and society's expectations of how we should conform. We are conditioned to believe that there is a certain kind of path to life – that we must go to school, college and university; be successful by working ten hours a day in a cubical. If that isn't enough, we are expected to meet someone before we get too old and pop out a few kids, obviously not before getting married first and having a big shiny wedding to make sure yours outdoes everyone else's.

This kind of a life does not scream passion, purpose or fulfilment to me. I am not saying there is anything wrong with doing those things in isolation if it is what you love. But the expectations the world has of us is a harsh burden to bear.

Through this constant conditioning, we ourselves then begin to put our own expectations out into the world. Believing that a boy or girlfriend should act like this, or a husband or wife should be like that. This is entangling ourselves in a place of misery until the day we die.

By relinquishing those expectations, I have been able to find inner peace and calm. I found there was no need for me to live up to anyone else's standards. For my soul is the only place that the truth resides.

I don't question how other people will behave or expect them to act in a certain way. I just explore life freely and I am always overjoyed with what I find. This takes away a lot of the previous anxiety and worries I suffered with before.

This isn't something you can achieve overnight, but having the awareness of the expectations is the most important point to remember.

The dust had begun to settle, it was a time of new beginnings. The energy was brewing - only a few months to go until the astrological operations of the Saturn Return would come into effect. The air was filled with the heat of summer. She was almost able to touch all the truth and expansion that was upon her. Slowly, slowly my child, one moment at a time. If you go too fast you will fall.

5

Heat of Summer

It was just like another normal Friday night. It was not a place where I usually danced but it was the first time I was able to salsa since injuring my knee that summer. I met my friends for dinner beforehand and we headed to the salsa social event afterwards. I saw him as soon as I entered the room.

His name was Diego. My sister had met him a couple of weeks before, so I already knew who he was as she had told me about him. He was new there. I could tell he had noticed me too and he asked me to dance. He was fun, energetic and easy to follow.

Our paths crossed again at the bar where he was talking to my friend and my initial observation was that he was arrogant, perhaps only for show. He was selling himself in an overconfident manner but I knew there was something else to him. This was just his way of getting people's attention and feeling them out.

After a few minutes of him playing some stupid games, we entered into a real conversation. With ease it became deep and meaningful, the salsa behind us faded into a blur until the DJ announced the last song.

He was different, I liked him despite thinking he was a bit

proud. He had an interesting take on life, one I wanted to explore.

He asked when we could continue the conversation, so I suggested "now?" He looked at me, stunned, unable to comprehend what I had said to him. My suggestion to live for the moment had surprised him. He quickly replied with an enthusiastic "yes". It was quite late, around 2:00 am, so we made our way to a café that was still open. We ordered some tea and continued our conversation.

I explained to him my current philosophy about the importance of the age twenty-eight and how my mum predicted this intense shift; detailing my current career situation and that my life had been turned upside down over the past seven months.

I also told him that despite how painful the growth was, it was necessary. I was ready to embrace whatever these changes meant for my life. In his words: 'this was a miracle for me'.

He was right, I was grateful to be woken.

He too had experienced a similar sense of awakening some years prior and he was very excited about my journey. He did not have the advanced knowledge and intellect of my Magical Metaphysical Man, but he knew more than me and I was curious to hear about his evolution.

::

The following week I met Diego for dinner and I was really excited. After all the struggles I had faced with Lex, I still remained a true romantic at heart and believed that love could conquer all.

We met on a Sunday night. It was a warm summer evening, and the restaurant was filled with people. But there was only us. We were in our little bubble and there was an instant connection which we could not deny.

Over dinner, he explained more to me about his time in Cuba, how that led to his progression and that despite moving to

London to pursue his career in banking he hadn't 'bought into' that kind of life. He described his time in Havana with great passion – the way I felt about India, I thought. We shared a quiet knowing, him more so than I, for he was aware of all the changes I was about to encounter. I, however, was quite ignorant of the journey ahead. I loved his thoughts about life. His philosophies were interesting and were very close to my own. When I shared with him my philosophy about love he agreed with me, and I could tell he was special.

As he was new to London he wanted me to share a piece of 'my' London with him. So after dinner we took a walk and the night sky was perfectly lit – it seemed that even the stars had come out to play with us. We walked side by side, closer and closer until he had his arms around me. He brushed my hair back from my face lightly and kissed my lips. It was magical. Whenever I was in his company time seemed to stand still; non-existent in our presence.

::

My final working day had come. I was twenty-four hours away from freedom. I didn't know how my life was about to evolve but I knew this moment was significant. After what seemed the longest day I packed up my belongings for the last time. Having almost killed myself in the quest for a career, it was time to break free of the chains I had been locked in for twelve years.

It was now time to be in pursuit of myself, to begin the journey inwards.

My final weekend at home was filled to the brim with love. It began late that Friday night with a family send-off. After years of wanting to take the leap and travel solo, it was really happening. My mother had bought me a travel journal for me to write all my thoughts. Little did she know that later down the road it would be the inspiration for this book.

The following day I was meeting Diego for my send-off date. He knew that this trip was incredibly special for me, and it was time for me to be alone. That meant I wouldn't be speaking to anyone during the next month, including him.

I had decided to take a vacation from all that 21st-century life expects of us. My intention was to live without my mobile phone for a month. No social media, no emails, no electronics. Just me exploring the world. I planned to remain in touch with my family during this time but I'd had enough of the constant phone addiction. I was done with it.

I wanted to create a peaceful space to be.

I had already been clearing out the excessive amounts of apps on my phone, in disbelief that each of these demanded my attention at some point during the day. How did I keep up with them all? I deleted outright a vast number of them that I felt did not serve me, leaving only the bare minimum. I also noted how many types of social media accounts I had. Did I really need them all? What were they all there for? Again I completed a process of removing that which did not serve me. In the end I was left with one social media account only. Surely one is all we require, if we even require one at all?

::

Diego arranged for us to meet for dinner at 7:00 pm. He met me at the tube station with a warm embrace. We walked hand in hand to the restaurant and sat outside in the light of the full moon. The twinkly lights amongst the lattice of branches and overgrown plants only added to the ambience. Despite it being a Saturday night at prime dining time, we had the whole space to ourselves. It was as if he planned it that way.

There was a present waiting on the table for me – a book called *The Power of Now* by Eckhart Tolle. Diego had bought it for me as a farewell present and I couldn't wait to begin reading it. He had shared how this book had changed his life and I hoped it would inspire change in my life also. I treasured his thoughtful gift.

The past week had been incredible. We had created some beautiful moments together, but it was short-lived. I was afraid to leave behind what we had created. Only in my dreams had I believed that what we were experiencing could be real. I was ready for my journey of self-discovery but I wanted to take him with me. Despite only knowing him for a short few weeks, I felt strongly in my heart that I had met my soulmate and that this would be the beginning of a new chapter for me in so many ways.

::

On my last evening in London, before everything became so startlingly different, I met my friends for dinner. We played, danced and chatted. I felt at home here. They were all so excited for my journey and I was surrounded by love. Even my friend from California made a virtual appearance.

S was my soul-sister. Even though we had met just four years ago it was as if I had known her for a lifetime and she came at the perfect time, just as I was breaking up with my ex. With her long, dark, shiny hair and laid-back Californian attitude, she was obsessed with travel, exploration and love as much as I was. We were connected at another level, one out of our control. She too had experienced a break up and that definitely bonded us further.

S was my favourite type of human being, she always had something beautiful to offer the world. She was there to lend an ear to listen or a shoulder to cry on when you needed it, but mostly I loved her for the way she saw the world. She breathed new light into things.

I honoured the way that even when she spoke of a negative individual or situation she would do it in the most positive of ways - something I continually aspire to get right.

::

After my break-up I had sought solace in the salsa world, using it as a place to escape my problems. During this time I had become part of a group that was, I felt, my salsa family. I spent all my free time with them during those last three months. After one more night of dancing with all my favourite people, it was time to say goodbye. It was hard to leave this part of my life and happiness behind.

    After two and half days of goodbyes, it was Monday morning and I had a flight to catch. I was off, off and away to Helsinki where it would all begin. All I had now was a backpack and unknown territory ahead of me. I had never lived in this uncertainty before.

Teaching on Soulmates

Important encounters are planned by the souls long before the bodies see each other. –Paulo Coelho

I believe we can have multiple soulmates. Some may be romantic in nature, others a brother or sister relationship, but ultimately these are people we feel deeply connected to at a higher level. A soulmate may appear for a short period of time to inspire us to grow or remind us who we are, or we may have the pleasure of them being with us for a large part of our journey.

Once you meet them you will know, because you will feel as if you have known them a hundred thousand years. You will wish you had met them sooner and you will wish they would stay with you forever. But you can guarantee that even if they do have to leave you, they will always hold a space in your heart that will keep you alive until you meet again.

They will be there throughout the good and the bad and it will be a bond like no other. Nothing will get in the way of them loving, supporting and inspiring you for the rest of your days. They will uplift you and raise you to your highest potential.

This life lesson is dedicated to my first true soulmate and my soul sister. A soul that enabled me to experience and gain the understanding of what a soulmate really is, and why they enter our lives. S you are a beautiful soul and I hope our friendship lasts infinite lifetimes.

Wander until you are lost, lose yourself for a while and then realise you were right there all along. Travel leaves you in a silence, a peace that cannot be altered until the day you are ready to return and share the stories. Explore sweet one, explore until your heart's content, find what you are searching for and then return home to us.

6

Exploring

As I landed in my first destination I realised how much suffering and pain I felt inside. It was time to heal wounds from the lies, the deceit and the conditioning of this ugly world. I needed to regain my energy so I would be able to continue along this path we call life.

After seven days of peaceful rest and wandering the streets of the Baltics, I had begun to feel at home in the world again. I was present, aware of the now. My feelings were no longer hidden in the depths of my soul. Some days I cried and wept for the sorrow I had stored up inside. The pain of my childhood, relationships that were not to be, the career and mess of my final days there – it all came pouring out.

It was as if I had looked inside, become aware of all of the dark I had left to fester and finally had the courage to deal with it. It was important for me to cleanse myself of the negative energy that was holding me back. It was time to accept, forgive and leave this firmly in the past. It was time to move forward.

The simplicity of my travelling days soothed my soul. I had few belongings and little money but this made me feel more alive than ever before. My only possessions were the clothes I wore and my backpack.

I began to understand that possessions only weigh us down. In the way I had experienced the lightness associated with becoming vegan, I felt the same about my belongings. Although I was not ready to return home yet, I knew when that day came I would continue to live as simply as I could.

::

I was fortunate enough to be able to connect with the most beautiful souls throughout my exploration.

First I met Oliver in a Health Food store and he provided me with a great itinerary to make the most of my time in Helsinki. Oliver was one of life's free spirits. I noticed him right away with his happy, full smile. Even though there was a pain behind his eyes he shined brightly. He later shared with me that the pain was due to his broken relationship and the separation he had to endure from his daughter.

Following his recommendation, I explored Suomenlinna, a tiny island just off of Helsinki and a UNESCO Heritage site. Suomenlinna dates back to World War Two and has beautiful views of Helsinki, along with its own historic landmarks, including the Kings Palace. The following afternoon was filled with music and friendship at an open-air Jazz festival which took place in Espalandi - one of my favourite spots in Helsinki.

Staying at my first hostel, I met Hayden from the USA. He was a quiet soul, and if I hadn't made the first move I doubt we would have been friends. In the dark, worn pizzeria below the hostel we began our conversation. He was kind, gentle and very honest with me. He shared that he had been struggling with bi-polar and that this trip was his opportunity to find his internal happiness so he could return home with a fresh start. I shared a similar story of how messy my life was back home, telling him that I longed to travel forever, for in this space was where I felt most free. He agreed.

I really appreciate that in my travels I met so many open people that were willing to go deep into conversation with me, to places most people wouldn't want to. This is one of my favourite elements of travelling alone.

In Tallinn, I met Johannes, who was between his internship and job and had decided to volunteer at the hostel to prevent boredom. I liked him right away. He was tall, dark and handsome. I enjoyed the way he looked at me, as if he saw more than the outside, physical body. It was as if he could see through straight into my soul.

We spent a whole rainy day together, first exploring Linnahall, a former concert and sports venue. It is situated on the harbour, just beyond the walls of the Old Town. For the entire thirty-minute walk, it poured with rain. We got lost and very wet. But we were determined to arrive at our destination and were not bothered by the weather. When Johannes said he was not good with directions he wasn't kidding. At home, I would have been desperate to reach my journey's end but here time seemed to stand still. I had no place to be and relaxed in the comfort of my schedule-free life.

Linnahall was breath-taking.

The views across the harbour and the Old Town will be etched in my memory forever, along with the moments that I shared on that wall with Johannes. Our connection was instantaneous, genuine and deep. We talked about our childhoods, past relationships and this thing we call life. A ladybug even stopped by to enjoy our conversation.

After a Vipassana meditation session (an ancient Indian meditation to see things as they really are, a process of self-purification by self-observation) that Johannes led me through, we carried on exploring in silence and walked the city wall, which is still wonderfully intact. Later we had dinner at the only vegan restaurant in Tallinn: Vegan Restoran V - followed by a tour of the beautiful city look-outs. The day took its own course and turned out to be perfectly dreamy.

This was the first time I had wanted to stay a little longer, but as Johannes said, "it's always best to leave on a high otherwise you'll ruin it". Something that would be useful to remember for the rest of my travels.

::

After exploring the Balkans I was ready to move to somewhere warmer where the Sun would shine all day long and where I would grow. I found myself in Seville, Spain where the Sun shone for eleven hours a day and the temperature was 40°C. I could not remember the last time I had actively chosen to learn something, something I really cared about. It was here in Seville that I began my Spanish studies. I loved the feeling of waking up in morning excited and enthusiastic. I couldn't wait to get to school and explore the city, practising my Spanish as I went.

One of my favourite things about Seville was the tiny streets; at the end of each was a beautifully placed monument. I was making great use of my Diana camera which had been gifted to me by S, instead of reaching for my smartphone I was back to basics. I fully immersed myself into the flow of Spanish life by taking my daily siesta and eating paella de verduras - my favourite Valencian rice dish with vegetables. After another day following my new ritual, I spent the early evening wondering the Parque de Maria Louisa which houses the Plaza de España. I spent hours there writing and taking in the surroundings, in the shade of course, like a true Sevillian.

I found it hugely therapeutic to write down the lessons I was learning each day. I realised that it was always possible to be growing from our experiences if we pay close attention and become aware of them.

::

I have always been in awe of those that could speak a second language. I saw this as such an incredible gift, but for a long time I never felt I would be able to achieve similar success. I used to excuse myself by replaying the age-old mantra: 'I don't have the time'. When I was handed the gift of time, I knew that I must allow myself the opportunity to begin.

Once disconnected from my phone I discovered that I was able to live in the moment without distraction. It enabled me to see how damaging this device had been for me. I rarely read nor did I spend time alone with my thoughts.

I was always reaching for my phone to occupy me, as if I

was incapable of occupying myself. I did not miss social media or the distraction of it all. It was liberating to be free of it. I carried my book in my bag and during moments of extended space I educated myself, the way we used to.

During this time I was able to reconnect with my true self – the real me, free of all the social and societal conditioning. My previously troubled mind was now at rest. The cobwebs had been cleared and I was living each day with a clarity I did not have before. I felt my personal power flowing through. My internal fire had been lit and from now on it was never going out. My thoughts shifted to the idea of life holding a purpose, something greater than ourselves. I wondered frequently what my purpose was, so I read up on the subject and asked many people their thoughts.

Some days I believed my purpose was to just be myself - to inspire others through my positive and happy nature. Those were the days I believed life is simple. On the days I thought too deeply into the subject, I exhausted myself with ideas and ultimately gave up, feeling it was all a bit too difficult to discover the truth.

The whole time I was away, I was seeking the answer to this burning question. Surely the corporate lifestyle wasn't all this world had to offer me? Irrespective of whether or not I knew my purpose, I still sought a new direction. The longer I was away, the harder it became to even think about returning. I knew there had to be another answer, another way. I wanted to fill my days with meaning, something that truly made my heart sing.

During these moments, my thoughts drifted to my Magical Metaphysical Man. I had many questions and knew he would have the answers. All in good time though, I thought, for now I was grateful to have the space to live at a much slower pace and I would embrace this opportunity. I knew he would return when my healing was complete. He knew I needed this time alone.

::

Attending Spanish school enabled me to make plenty of friends during my stay. On one occasion, there was a long holiday weekend so a group of us visited Cadiz. We stopped for brunch at a place called Cafe Royalty which had been open since 1912. Our waitress Bea was the spirit of the café. She was so patient - especially when she had four people attempting to speak Spanish. It was what we all referred to as 'the last meal' and was the kind of brunch where, if you never lived to eat another meal, you'd be okay with it.

The time had come for me to continue my travels further south. It was especially sad to say goodbye to Nico, my Parisian friend, whom I had formed a strong connection with and who had been part of the group to Cadiz. However, I knew I would be seeing him again soon. We delved into all subjects and explored them, especially those surrounding love. He had come across some relationship issues while we were away and I had offered a shoulder to cry on.

Goodbyes are always hard, no matter how many times you go through them. I was beginning to understand that this is the nature of life, the natural coming and going. In the 21st century we attempt to hold onto everything we have, never allowing ourselves to let go. Despite feeling sadness in the moment, I knew that with every goodbye I would invite a new hello.

Teaching on Human Connection

I have been privileged and blessed to encounter many different human beings during my travels and over the course of my life. It never ceases to amaze me what we are able to learn from others if we have an open mind. While travelling I connected with some of the most beautiful beings on the planet, beings that have left me speechless when they shared their journey with me.

It was apparent that we all have our own journey through life.

It is easy to judge another culture when you do not understand it but it is important that we learn from each other. My heart has been opened to many countries and cultures that do not reflect a British way of life and I believe this contributes to my ability to be compassionate. Through the ability to understand other cultures we are able to connect with a greater number of people and that it is what we are here to do.

Feel connection...

It is an absolute requirement in order for us to live happily. We are beings who strive for and seek connection, love and belonging. We must put aside the judgement, so we can enjoy each other's presence, for we do not know how long we will be blessed with it.

She was growing through the loneliness. A wildflower incapable of being restrained, expanding in all directions; the only way now was up. The journey of the soul started with the Sun work and here she would have the Sun in abundance. She would also find enlightenment in learning a new language and what it means to connect and communicate on a deeper level.

7

Magic Island

My Spanish exploration continued from Seville through to the wondrous magical island of Ibiza, where a part of my heart still remains today. When I first arrived I had no expectations. I had been there before so I was relaxed in my approach. My time in Spain had certainly had a calming effect on me, and I was becoming later for each event in true Spanish style. Time seemed to be non-existent to me, whereas before I was constantly clock watching.

I noticed during my travels how locked up in labels I was. Even though I enjoyed wearing some of them, they were becoming so much a part of me. If we are not careful we can become stuck in our boxes and no longer able to find our way out. Before we know it we are out of options. I was gradually tearing away all of the layers to reveal myself. I was no longer defined by a label, I was free. It was a beautiful feeling to release myself from the boxes I had previously lived in.

In some ways I fell off the rails for a little while, drinking fruity cocktails by the beach side and eating sugar to my heart's content. These poisons were not typical of my diet back home but I felt rebellious at this point even though I knew this would not be serving my body in the long run, I wanted to break free from myself for a little while. I wanted to do just as I pleased, and sometimes that is an equal form of nourishment.

Everyone I met was a stranger, so I had the freedom to be whoever I wanted to be. It was helpful for me to speak with honesty and not feel judged, or care if I was being judged - especially at a time when I was growing. I was able to speak of my life's experiences and evolving philosophies in a carefree manner.

::

My happiness in learning a new language continued and I loved the feeling of communicating with a different culture in their mother tongue. It was an experience I had never had before. The joy when I connected sentences and was able to communicate with those I previously could not speak to made my heart sing. I was encouraged and motivated to continue with my new found passion. During this time I found that I had a new dream: to speak Spanish fluently.

The Sun drenched me in its healing rays and the energy of Ibiza lifted me up. It was here that for the first time I felt I had come home. My heart had been stolen by this island. I had never experienced such an intense pull, but Ibiza had made up her mind, I belonged to her. I belonged there.

It was then I realised that when you think you have it all figured out, everything changes. I've realised in life you cannot commit to anything forever, because nothing is eternal, not even our thoughts. In the time it takes to hold one conversation you can have a completely fresh outlook on life and how you want to live it.

Ibiza was a huge learning experience for me. I looked around and saw that there were people not only living here, but they were thriving. The love and sense of community was beautiful. Ibiza is sometimes misunderstood – seen as a party island, full of drugs and mayhem, but I never knew it like that. I knew it for its pure, natural beauty. I knew it for the life force energy that refreshed my soul and healed my wounds.

I became whole again there.

As the Sun shone brightly on Ibiza, I continued each day to draw the specific dimensional frequencies from it, as my Magical Metaphysical Man had taught me. The more I practised them, the more I noticed a sense of expanded consciousness, a sense of health and positivity.

Our emotions play a huge part in terms of whether we have a high or low frequency. Emotional states such as happiness, joy, gratitude, and love are conducive to a higher frequency (expanded) consciousness and good health. However, when we experience negative feelings such as pain, sadness, anxiety, or fear we operate within a lower frequency range of (compressed) consciousness which not only blocks our highest-life potentials, but also opens the door to disease.

Life became easier and easier. The right opportunities presented themselves to me and it was as if every move I made was applauded by the Universe in line with my path. I was in the flow of life; I was experiencing a sense of being as described in Eckhart Tolle's *The Power of Now*.

::

And so it began, a new direction; I found that I didn't want just a new dream, I wanted a new life. I wanted to spend my days at the beach, having fun with friends from all over the world, not wasting my life away in a stuffy office with a bunch of suits working on meaningless tasks.

I wanted to change the world; I wanted to be of value and inspire others.

When I think about what I wanted to do, how I felt and how, logically, it was insane to give up my 'career' to live at the beach, it made no sense at all. But at the same time it made a lot of sense. Since when did my career bring me true fulfilment and happiness anyway? You know, the kind where you jump out of bed in the morning raring to go.

The beach, however, always brought me joy. Mother Nature is able to provide us with all of the essence of life through her natural resources.

::

After a late night out in Ibiza town and having met a group of excited strangers from New York, we decided to do the only thing that you should do at 5:00 am - watch the sunrise. I shared a beautiful moment with one of the guys from New York as the Sun peeked above the ocean and collided with the clouds to create a beautifully lit red morning sky. Our conversation began with our pure undistracted desire to watch the sunrise. We shared very few words. This was the essence of living in the moment. Living through experience. One look was all it took to know the bond was special.

I was blessed and began to think about the moments that I had recently been experiencing with other human beings. To get so deep with someone you've known for just an hour or so didn't seem to happen in my life in London. I craved this depth. Surface conversations seemed a waste of time.

I quickly realised that London wasn't the problem; it was the frequency I was stuck on there. Everyone I seemed to meet along my travels had the same energy frequency as me and I seemed to be attracting one interesting soul after the other. I guess it all depends on where you are in your life. In London, I was with people that lived the same mundane life as I did; working, paying rent... existing. But now I was truly living, this was the feeling I was longing for.

To live is the rarest thing in the world. Most people just exist.
– Oscar Wilde

To me, these people were all living the dream. They seemed to have an authenticity and were doing what they loved.

They weren't adhering to some social expectation of how much money they should be earning or what their job title was.

::

As I landed in Valencia I found myself resisting it. My physical body had flown across the sea and landed on fresh, new unexplored soil. My heart, however, was hopelessly in love and left behind in Ibiza. I tried to reclaim it but it was a lost cause. But heart or no heart I was only in Valencia for a few days and I vowed to enjoy it while I could.

Later that day I met two Canadian girls who I took to eat paella. We drank sangria and chatted. They were only young and I felt as if they looked to me for some wisdom about travelling, so I shared my latest teachings with them. I told them of my burning desire to understand my purpose and how I was searching within myself for the answers. I explained to them that they must follow their hearts and never be afraid to carve their own path. I also expressed my love for Ibiza and my dreams for the future.

The waiter overheard that I had fallen in love with Ibiza and kept making jokes about how Valencia was better. In order to win my affection for his city he gave us free shots of Mastella, a very sweet wine, and the most delicious Spanish drink I had ever tried. The girls told me about a local Spanish market close by and we agreed to go in the morning before my Spanish classes. The market was filled with fruit and vegetable stalls with fresh juices - everything from mango and kiwi juice to freshly made gazpacho; being vegan was easy here.

The Valencian beach stretched for miles, but since the Spanish were on their summer vacations it wasn't easy to find a good spot with a clear view of the ocean. The more time I spent in the Sunshine and on the beach, the more I didn't want to go back to dull London weather.

I felt good in the Sunshine and I was convinced that these natural wonders of the world were what filled me up with peace, love and energy.

A new found friend at the hostel was obsessed with a typical Valencian drink called Horchata, so we walked the full stretch of the beach to try this delicious nut milk. The freezing cold drink was so refreshing in the warm summer heat, I had two.

::

A month into my journey, I celebrated by facing a fear. I had always been afraid of the sea and never felt like a strong swimmer, but I overcome some of this whilst in Xabia. Xabia is a seaside town a few hours' drive from Valencia.

My comfort level for swimming was typically about a metre away from the shore, but on this day I swam about 350 metres out to a little platform. It felt amazing to overcome this fear, which I had been holding onto for a long time. It doesn't mean the fear had fully dissipated but it was a great start. It was a wonderful experience to push myself and realise the possibilities of my power.

I will hold onto this moment in the knowledge that all fear can be eliminated. We just have to find a reason to overcome it.

Teaching on Heart Feelings

I could never have planned to fall in love with Ibiza. I had been once before but this time I had an energetic pull that was impossible for me to ignore. Every part of my body longed for me to return, yet I had not really left. I missed places I hadn't seen and I was hopelessly in love with a place I barely knew.

I believe that feelings are far more valuable than our thoughts, so if you feel you have a resonance with something, do not deny yourself that pleasure. Go with the feeling. Our feelings are a key; whether positive or negative they speak to us.

Sometimes we instinctively feel something that is beyond the mind to comprehend and my advice is to go with that feeling. Why do we always need a reason for everything? Isn't it enough to just 'feel' it?

I was overcome with feeling everything that Ibiza had to offer me: beautiful souls, Sunshine, beaches, and freedom to be away from the world I had lived in for so long, the world where I felt forced to conform. Sometimes the heart knows things that the mind could never explain.

Whatever steals your heart, do that. You will regret it if you don't.

She was not about to find love in the way she believed it could be found. She was about to discover her first philosophy of life. It would come to her purely, with ease. As if the idea had been planted in her mind while she slept, awakening in the morning to discover a whole new meaning to life.

8

𝒪

In Valencia, I stumbled across my very first philosophy of life. I had come to notice that life was a circle, a constant flow of connected energy. The flow of creation to death, from day to night, from love to hate and everything in between was 𝒪 - this eternal circular energy pattern which repeats itself. Each experience gives birth to a polar opposite: the positive and the negative, if you will, and each side always comes back around to begin anew. Thus, the circle of life means all is one.

I found this circular energy repeating itself during my travels as I journeyed from one place to the next. I would notice that as I said hello to one soul, I would say goodbye to another. I disliked the comings and goings at first. It was only after experiencing this cycle a number of times and allowing the powers of the Universe to be, that I discovered this eternal flow of circular energy. I noticed how this could be applied to all things in my life.

In the beginning, I wanted to control how I kept these people in my life but it was no use trying to hold onto these connections or fighting to keep that person by my side. The journey is not about holding on, it is about letting go.

In modern life I feel that we have many tools to stay connected with precious souls and acquaintances. These tools counteract the balance of the Universe by continuing to connect us to that which we were supposed to leave. I do not believe that we are supposed to be eternally connected to anything. We are supposed to live freely in the eternal bliss of the universal cosmic powers, allowing that which will be... to be.

This constant need to control and hold on prevents us from moving forward in life and letting go of a past which does not serve us. Each experience we encounter will be different, therefore we must enjoy the moment with gratitude for being able to learn something from another soul or enjoy a moment in time with them. Then we must release them back to the Universe for someone else to enjoy, allowing both parties to continue forth on their path.

It's all about the flow of life. In order for something new to enter our life, something else must leave. The Universe likes to fill empty spaces. We soon realise this is the eternal flow of our human experience. Never be sad for what is lost, as it can always be found again. We are continuously in the process of the never-ending ☉, because even after death comes rebirth; and through the darkness came light, not the other way around.

::

I discovered later in my cosmic studies that this philosophy was also known as the 'Eternal Return' or the 'Eternal Recurrence', represented by the ancient symbol of a serpent eating its tail, constantly re-creating itself. This symbol represents the circular nature of all things; cycles that begin once again.

This Eternal Recurrence is noted in the conclusion of the physician-philosopher Sir Thomas Browne's 17th Century book, *The Garden of Cyrus*:

"All things began in Order, so shall they end, and so shall they begin again."

O

::

Whilst in Barcelona, during a conversation with new friends I was fascinated to discover that our bodies renew themselves every seven years. I was advised that if you are in tune with your body you will be able to feel or sense the change. This increased my belief that twenty-eight was a number of significance. Ever since I had turned twenty-eight I had felt as though I had been reborn, which would make sense if my body had completely renewed itself.

This led me to understand the importance of the number seven and how the number seven always represented a complete set.

For example:

- Days of the week
- Notes in the Musical scale
- Primary colours of the rainbow
- Classical planets
- Alchemical metals

::

Unfortunately, some things are not meant to be, regardless of expectations or wishful thinking. This new philosophy of life would come in useful, particularly with regards to my relationship with Diego. Sadly, we were over before we had really had the chance to begin.

It surprised me because I truly felt that Diego was journeying along a not too distant path from my own, and I had felt quite sure that we were a match made to be. So I was disappointed when it drew to an end and although it hurt to think of what could have been, it was necessary.

Relationships shine a mirror back on us, exposing all the parts we don't like about ourselves. It is up to us to work through these experiences in a productive way when they show up. Otherwise, the same lesson will keep haunting us.

I would never know or understand why, but Diego and I vanished in a blink of an eye. Unfortunately, my new skills seemed to stop short at matters of the heart and I could never quite seem to get it right. Despite this longing to spend my days as part of a couple, I vowed to let the Universe determine my fate if I was to be blessed with a soulmate.

::

After wandering through Alicante, Madrid and Barcelona I returned to the Magic Island. My Magic Island - Ibiza. The connection I felt there was beyond my imagination, it was indescribable and the entire two weeks between my visits had felt like an eternity.

It didn't matter how many days I had travelled, how many places I had visited or who I met along the way; my mind had expanded beyond my greatest expectations. In some ways, I was still beautifully lost, because I had died to the old goals and dreams I had set for myself.

Now I was open and ready to set out new dreams which were simple, unconventional and unexpected. There were so many questions unanswered, so many possibilities; so many paths that I could now take and only time would tell my destiny.

Sadly, society conditions us to believe that the way to achieve happiness is typically through careers, money and possessions. But I now knew there was a different way to achieve happiness. It was driven from the inside and once I tapped into this, it was mine forever.

::

Every day I spent researching and exploring my Magic Island, the more it became like home to me. I couldn't explain why, but I'd never felt so at peace in a place I barely knew.

I was staying in a wonderful abode with an enchanting soul who seemed to host only the most beautiful-hearted guests, most of whom were only staying for a few days at a time. It felt terrible when they left, but I was always pleased when the next bunch arrived. To learn from these other beautiful creatures from around the world was my favourite pastime. Many an hour was spent in that blue kitchen talking about life, love and dreams.

During my stay I met a charming Parisian photographer, a natural beauty with long flowing dark locks. She fell in love with my blue dress and asked to photograph me - in my blue dress, in the blue kitchen. How could I resist an opportunity like that? I agreed with pleasure and one lazy afternoon we began the process of capturing these blue moments. After getting to know each other, it unfolded that she was on a journey too. She had given up her previously boring job and discovered her passion for photography. I was immediately inspired by her bravery to pursue a life filled with purpose. I hoped that I too would be able to find mine - sooner rather than later.

It was necessary for the Universe to place these types of individuals in my life in order for me to learn. To understand that these travelling moments were not just for healing, resting and fun but that it was all very much part of the process of discovering myself.

Time away from my previously dull corporate job that was sucking the life out of me, enabled me to see how stressed and how unhappy I had been before. This journey was allowing me the space to understand that I didn't just need a holiday. I needed a new life.

I entertained myself with new friends, beach days and reading for hours on end. At the top of Ibiza Old Town there was an open-air Jazz festival that filled my evenings with great pleasure. The sea breeze on top of the hill added to the shivers that went down my spine as the artists played.

::

The first time I encountered 'smudging' was during my stay in that wonderful home. Tessa, the enchanting host, came home one day and was preparing things for the next guest. This was when I saw her clear the energy from the home. It was a divine moment, where the energy of past humans dissipated and the energy within the space was renewed.

I welcomed the experience, thinking of my Magical Metaphysical Man in the process and wondering where he was, knowing he was sure to have something to say on this subject.

Later I discovered that "smudging" (the burning of particular aromatic herbs to fill a room with smoke and then ventilating it) was a typical Native American practice that helps to purify or clear out negative energy from a space. This can be very useful if you have any unwelcome residual energy from visitors or occupants of your home and is an effective way to renew the energy quickly.

::

The Universe kept me in Ibiza as long as I needed. I felt my time there was inadequate but I knew I had made plenty of progress. Despite my longing to stay, my healing was complete. It was now time to return home; it was time to discover my purpose.

Teaching on Disappointment

Disappointment adds to the growth of the soul. It stems from an over expectation and not living in the moment. How many of us have encountered disappointment?

It's a fact of life that occasionally we have setbacks and delays or as in my experience, disappointment for 'what could have been'.

If you are struggling with disappointment you are living in the past, holding onto something that could have been, but wasn't. You will find that by shifting your energy and thoughts to the now, you can remove yourself from the pain.

By living in the now we can be fully present and available to enjoy life and experience it. If we allow ourselves to be present in each moment, we will experience the true joy that life has to offer. We are human so we can't expect life to be perfectly positive in every way, but we can expect that life unfolds as it should.

The disappointments are usually to steer us in the right direction to something that will be far more beneficial to us. Allow yourself to feel the pain, acknowledge it and then move forward, returning to reality and living in the moment.

And in a flash, she was back where she started.
But she would never be the same again.

9

The Return

On returning to London I was met with open, loving arms by my family and friends who had missed me so. I was blessed to be surrounded by so much love once again. Others could tell my energy was renewed. My family were pleased to see me, to see me glowing with happiness and being myself. I had been disconnected from myself before I left and even I noticed how 'me' I was being. My mum announced that she had never seen me so happy and alive. I was certain that it was the healing powers of the Sun.

I had left Ibiza behind and escaped the sinking feeling I expected to have. Although I was sad to leave, I knew I would be back. Now was the time for me to celebrate and embrace this exciting moment. I had found myself; I finally knew who I was inside. Although I had only been gone for two months, the healing process felt as though it had taken two years.

On my return, everything came together and I realised how much I had grown and changed as a person during my time away. Some of us never have this opportunity as we are far too distracted by the constant noise and drama that the world presents us with.

If we all spent a little more time getting to know ourselves we would find out beautiful, wonderful things that we could have never imagined to be possible.

These distractions take away our focus and attention from creating the important things in life and gaining knowledge about who we really are. This is why I believe we are here - to understand our complexity and fulfil the purpose of our higher self.

If you practise stillness through meditation and quieten down, you will be able to hear the message from your soul. The voice is always there within us as our inner teacher, but it's up to us to choose whether or not to listen. I was grateful to find my voice and be able to listen and find the inner peace that is available to us through diving a little deeper.

The answers are always inside.

::

I was still curious about one specific question. The question that I am certain every human asks themselves at one point in their life. What is my purpose?

The more I thought about this question the more tangled my thoughts became. I had spent a lot of time during my travels thinking about this and looking for places where I added value. I knew I was a positive, happy person but that didn't equate to a new career - at least not in the way I was seeing the world.

I would have been quite happy to fall off the face of the earth and live off-grid in some kind of unspoilt land, but it seemed my destiny was to stay for a while. Life was as easy as could be whilst I was away, but it was at home in London that I would discover what my mission was. It would not unfold quickly though; this would be a slow unveiling of my path.

I knew in the depths of my soul I was here for a purpose bigger than I could fathom at that time. My mind wandered through the possibilities, but they all seemed too 'normal' somehow. I felt as if there was something so much more, something bigger than myself.

I began to take every test I could find on the internet, ones that are supposed to help you 'find your purpose now' or answer 'one question that will help realise your dream life'. I did find some of them to be useful or interesting, as they helped to solidify my own internal beliefs and values.

But the problem I found with these tests was, despite offering me some thoughtful processes to go through, they did not bring me closer to realising my actual purpose. I was already thoughtful. I was already in tune with my soul. I just couldn't seem to speak the words my inner self was trying to tell me. I trusted that my purpose would follow but I knew the more I sought or pushed for the answer the longer it would take to receive the information. I needed to practise the art of patience.

::

I kept a small shell by my bed. Each night before I shut off my night lamp, I looked at that shell and visualised the day when I would be living in my beach home, taking my daily walks beside the sea and enjoying the beautiful orange, glowing sunsets. The shell had a deep significance because I had picked it up on the beach in Ibiza and one day when I was clearing out my travelling backpack it tumbled out onto the floor with some unexpected sand from my beloved Cala Comte beach.

This tiny, perfectly formed, shell was a memory; a moment in time, a piece of my paradise island. It was something that represented all the growth I had achieved so far and all the growth I still had left to complete. It also served as a daily reminder of the dream I had.

Unfortunately, other people's negativity and judgement of my new dreams and outlook on life became quite hurtful. It made me feel as though I was incapable of making a sound decision. I am twenty-eight, I thought, if I cannot make a life decision now, when will I ever be able to?

What really rattled me was that half the people saying these things had never chased a dream in their life.

This chapter is dedicated to the dream chasers, the risk takers and those who believe in themselves. Those who know themselves and know they can do more.

Sometimes we humans believe we are teeny-tiny, but we are great. We are magnificent, beautiful, loving creatures and the possibilities are endless.

It is important that we learn to master ourselves and practise the art of self-containment. This is a continuing practice of mine and it is vital. Self-containment ensures that you do not allow the opinions or thoughts of others to dirty your inner guidance. If you have a dream or a purpose it is better to keep this inside, safe from those with opinions that can harm you. Your destiny is already made, so follow **your** path.

Destiny is a feeling you have that you know something about yourself nobody else does. The picture you have in your own mind of what you're about will come true. It's a kind of a thing you kind of have to keep to your own self, because it's a fragile feeling, and you put it out there, then someone will kill it. It's best to keep that all inside. - Bob Dylan

Teaching on the Meaning of Home

The best journey always takes us home.

I saw this quote printed on a wall in Valencia and it bothered me greatly. I couldn't understand the meaning of it and I realised that it was the use of the word 'home' which disturbed me. It wasn't until I understood the meaning of it, that I was able to understand the quote.

For me home is no longer a place, it is something we create within ourselves. Our own certainty gives us peace, clarity and a sense of belonging. Therefore, you can be anywhere in the world and still be at home.

The Universe provides our foundation, and the people in it give us all the love we need. We must be open to finding it and having more than you ever dreamed possible.

My extended travels taught me this important lesson, and I began to fall in love with the idea that home could be more than just the place you were born and grew up in. To me travelling the world was where I found my haven.

Part II

Her teacher led the way, guiding her towards her purpose; enabling her to delve further into the mysterious world of metaphysics. Once inside she would be handed the golden key.

10

Purpose

It was time to be reunited with my Magical Metaphysical Man. Over the past three months I had thought of him often. In some moments I felt the need to shy away from that which I knew he would teach me - some day or another. I even felt as though I should never see him again. But I couldn't hide now, it was too late and I had opened the can of worms. I was so out of my depth with metaphysics. I could never really be ready for this next step and I constantly questioned myself if this was the right thing to do, to follow this path. My upbringing had been religious until I was around ten and then became somewhat spiritual when my mum had found *The Secret* when I was in my late teens, which quickly became her new 'bible'.

I was open to learning and was always curious at heart which is probably how the next part of the story came around...

My Magical Metaphysical Man was back and it felt as though no time had passed since our last meeting. I explained to him how I was keen to discover my purpose and that I desperately wanted to move on from my usual 9-5 boring job and live a life of fulfilment. It was a waste of my breath though, since he already knew this information.

Before I had the chance to question him, he was already

preparing me for one of the most exciting journeys of my life. This would be a journey to discover the answer to the one question that had burned a hole in my thoughts over the past three months.

I was led into a type of out of body meditation, a technique where my consciousness was guided to another dimension – the 12th Dimension, in fact. It was indescribable. If you practice meditation you know the pure joy and peace it brings, so imagine this times 100!

He guided me to a place within the centre of the earth where I was first met by a spiritual being from my own soul family. I was taken by "Merkaba" light vehicle up through higher dimensional planes, up through the higher harmonic universes which exist beyond the frequency bands of our own. I watched in amazement as we passed through fields of gold, silver, blue-black, and then silver-black light, until we arrived in a field of pure white light.

My Magical Metaphysical Man issued an instruction, upon which a pillar of silver-white light appeared in front of me. A tall light-being stepped forward from the pillar.

"This is the Avatar level of your own consciousness," explained Magical Metaphysical Man "the portion of your own multi-dimensional identity stationed within the liquid light reality fields of the 12th dimension. Take its hands in yours and ask your questions telepathically. You will receive the answers or a sense of immediate knowing directly in your mind."

I couldn't help but notice the energy of love and peace radiating from this being. My higher soul connection had been re-established. It was here that I asked my burning question: what is my purpose?

After travelling back to this dimension, I came back to Earth with a bump.

"Are you okay?" he asked, concerned.

"Yes," I replied, "I just need a moment to readjust to this reality".

I was startled to say the least and struggling to ground my consciousness back into its normal space-time location. This was an experience like no other. It may have only lasted twenty minutes, but I wanted to stay for longer. I wanted to experience more. It was impossible to transmit into words the messages I had received but I clearly felt the intended direction of my soul. I had no idea how it would manifest itself but I trusted what I had felt that day.

Despite being scared before participating in this meditation, I now had no fear of him or his peculiar techniques. I was sold. I later replayed the event over and over and over in my head - it worked and I didn't need more proof than that. I was fully aware that if I shared the details of this with most people they would think I was barking mad. Even I questioned myself, but it was true and it was my experience – even if it was so out there it might sound like I made it up.

::

"On the matter of purpose, we should refer to the plants and flowers. A flower does not question its purpose here, it grows perfectly into what it should be, with no distractions or delays" explained my Magical Metaphysical Man.

He continued, warming to the theme: *"The plant and flower devas have an absolute (and joyful) purity of focus in the manifestation of their divine essence.[7] This, in part, is why we feel uplifted in their presence. The same process applies to humans. Those we find to be charismatic and original – the trend-setters – are simply expressing more faithfully the nature and purpose of their soul. By contrast, those who become entrained by the herd, those who slavishly follow the latest trends and fashions (whether these relate to politics, clothes, music, or haircuts) are displaying an essential **emptiness**, an essential disconnection from their own soul".*

Every time he appeared in my life he directed me on my path. It was as if he was my personal white knight, shining the light on my pathway. At any point I came to a crossroads and

---

[7] Deva meaning the higher dimensional intelligent archetype of consciousness which projects each species of plant and flower into manifestation within our reality field.

was unsure which way to go, he provided me with the insight to take the right turning.

Before I met him I was lost. My road map and soul connection had been taken from me. I had not understood my truly unlimited power, but he had been redirecting me to my higher purpose and expanding my consciousness. As he departed that day, we hugged goodbye as I knew I would not see him again for some time. It was then I knew of his special powers. The hug sent electrical currents through my body. Who was he? I was not sure I would ever really find out. By this point, it was too late to question him. Even if I wanted to know more, I doubted he would share it with me - that was not the purpose of his presence in my life.

::

My quest for true spiritual knowledge came after this cosmic adventure. Although I had previously suspected that all the answers were inside, I had now seen with my own eyes that they indeed were. This gave me a quiet confidence, as I knew every question held an answer that I would now be able to access. As long as I remained connected to my soul, the rest would flow effortlessly. I was hooked on this powerful, life-changing perspective.

I had a thirst for knowledge like never before. I wanted to understand all of the secrets of the Universe, and I knew my Magical Metaphysical Man would be able to help me.

I spent endless hours speaking with him, always starting our conversation with a new question which we would dissect. Usually I would end up with a whole list of fascinating new topics to research.

I had a stack of books to read and each time I read one, I found another dozen more to add to my reading list[8]. I had an obsession and I wanted to understand it all. The more I learned, the more I realised how much I had to learn and that this was in fact not the end, but the beginning of a very long quest.

---

[8] Refer to Bibliography.

I trusted that he would be able to take me far in my cosmic studies. He was my confidant, my guru, my guide. He made me feel less alone in a world where the majority of us are happily burying our heads in the sand never truly understanding the world as it is.

Some days I feared he would disappear, vanishing into thin air and I would be left thinking this was all some kind of mysterious dream, trying to prove to the world he was real, as if I had some made up an imaginary friend that no-one else could see.

I felt concerned that without him I would be forever alone. The more I changed, the harder it was to engage in normal human activities such as watching the television, discussing the news or drinking myself into oblivion – activities I never enjoyed even before him. But now everything felt dull in comparison to what I was learning. I was beginning to understand the world in a different way.

I felt like I was in on a secret, but it was so secret, even I didn't understand it myself.

All of a sudden I had become this new being, no longer wrapped up in 'worldly' affairs. I was questioning everything! I remember on one occasion, whilst meeting with my Magical Metaphysical Man, he delivered a whole host of truths to me. I was not, in fact, ready to take them on. They were about the sad state of our world and these details disappointed me, for I had always tried to keep a positive outlook on life.

That night I couldn't sleep, so perplexed by my thoughts. I questioned if what he had told me was true, but I couldn't understand why he would share something like that with me. This wasn't a game to him and I valued his direct brutal honesty, even if it hurt my sensitive nature.

I still regularly questioned if I should be spending time with him because I was changing so much. I was becoming a lion amongst the sheep and it was a daunting place to be, however often I thought these thoughts, I could never bring myself to stop. I was fascinated by it all.

Once I started down this spiritual path I realised that not all of us are on it. We have to evolve at our own pace. I personally believe it is something we all experience – a shift, a change, a spiritual encounter with a guru or with religious faith. Something that enters our life where we have an 'aha!' moment and change direction.

Still, this made me feel very uncomfortable and at a loss. My friendship circle had to evolve in order for me to grow and it was sad letting go of friends. I was becoming more and more isolated and I was afraid. When discussing this with my Magical Metaphysical Man he questioned if I would ever go back? The question was easy to answer: "no". I couldn't possibly pretend I didn't know these beautiful, strange things about the world. Life was exciting now and the techniques changed the course of my life, I would never give that up.

:::

The more knowledge I gained through reading and listening to my Magical Metaphysical Man, the more knowledge I sought. Each time, our encounters would cover another new topic.

His teachings started with nutrition and herbs, which provided me with a strong foundation. As he would say, "vegans are halfway there" because the commencement of spiritual evolution often begins with the diet. It was true for me that this expansion of consciousness came only with my shift towards raw, living vegetarian foods.

He had his own weird way of constructing 'planetary tea' which I found fascinating. By using the planetary vibration of each herb he was able to direct it to a specific part of the body. He explained: *"The physical body is really a holographic construct of light and sound, a system of energy patterns. Much like the colours of the rainbow (or notes in a musical scale), these energies can be reduced to seven primary "tones". The ancient philosophers correctly attributed these primary energetic (and planetary) tones to the various organs of the body. Thus, the liver was said to correspond to the vibration of Jupiter; the knees and bones were said to correspond to the vibration of Saturn, etc. By selecting a herb with the correct energetic quality, one can therefore strengthen and support specific organs in the body."*

The blends that he recommended came with strange instructions about when to take them and I recall him explaining that one particular tea should be taken in the "hour of the Sun", which happened to be at 3:00 am. Who drinks tea at 3:00 am? Well, I guess that would be me.

He provided me with a special 'all purpose' blend of seven herbs – one herb for each planet. Soon after I began taking this I felt the wonderful healing effects. Day to day life can be tiring, but with this blend, I found I had more energy. If I went a day or two without it, I felt the lack of nutrients. Previously, if I would have to spend a number of hours on a computer, I would suffer from headaches or migraines. After taking this blend, which included agrimony, the headaches and migraines became a thing of the past.

I also experienced positive effects after drinking a cup of yarrow tea in the morning to assist with irregular menstruation and painful periods; Yarrow is extremely beneficial for the reproductive organs of women. Abbé Kneipp says in his writings:

"Women could be spared many troubles if they just took Yarrow tea from time to time."

I began to experiment with various different herbal tea blends, understanding and feeling the power of the herbs, healing, cleansing and providing nutrients to the body.

I studied Maria Treben's *Health through God's Pharmacy: Advice and Proven Cures with Medicinal Herbs*. I was shocked that many ailments could be cured easily (and cheaply) with herbs.

From here, I was led naturally to discover the effects of Schuessler's tissue salts and homeopathic remedies. Before long, the pharmaceutical drugs I had once relied upon became a thing of the past. My diet was clean with fresh, living foods, I was practising herbal medicine and I was able to identify my own cures.

There was no need for me to pop pills like I used to. The answer was not in a pill – not long term anyway. Pills only provided a quick fix which potentially further damaged the body, creating more dis-ease. If I had an ailment I wanted to cure it at the root.

::

After a particularly testing day where the world was too much for me to bear, I sought comfort in my Magical Metaphysical Man. His mystical ways calmed and soothed my soul, for his frequency had that effect on humans.

A new exercise was presented to me, something he referred to as an 'Energy Shield', which could be used to protect and stabilize emotions. Soon after practising this I noticed how I had become relaxed and the troubles of my mind seemed to disappear. I began to practise this daily, to ensure that outside influences from the world had no effect on me. The more I practised, the longer the shield would last and the longer its soothing effects could be felt.

::

With his guidance, I was able to discover the effects of music on our consciousness. I had always been an 'old soul' at heart, fond of record players and jazz music which had served me well as I began to understand the powers of music more deeply.

He explained to me: *"Music has the power to raise our frequency. Listen to Bach, Handel, Mozart, Hayden or Vivaldi, for example, and they will lift you up. Listen to heavy bass rap music with derogatory words (or, in fact, most music which is electronic or digital in its instrumentation, recording and production) and you will lower your frequency instantaneously (even if you like it)."*

Some time back, long before my journey began I had stopped listening to the hard core, heavy metal I was once into – despite enjoying this type of music. I had noted the negative side-effects it had on me; it had the power to make me feel heavy with emotion and sadness.

It was then I knew that my choice of music required the same awareness that I applied to my food, considering carefully the ingredients to ensure I was not consuming anything that would have a negative impact on my health. I wanted to be a mindful consumer of all things that would have an impact upon my consciousness.

My musical exploration allowed me to discover the work of true artists: Handel, Bach, Vivaldi, Alessandro Piccinini, Charlie Christian, Bob Dylan, and Django Reinhardt. I then fell in love with lute music.

At school and at home I had received little exposure to these musical geniuses. I grew up surrounded by popular music and despite veering off the beaten path with Henry Mancini, Benny Goodman and Ray Charles, I was still lacking the musical knowledge that my Magical Metaphysical Man supplied me with. I had an appreciation of how important a part in metaphysics music plays. I was also beginning to understand the absolute significance of sound through other sources than my own personal experiences.

Jennifer Gehl in *The Science of Planetary Signatures in Medicine* explains:

"Plato believed that certain music could have deleterious effects on the soul and society.' She continues: *'Pythagoreans used certain forms of music to heal and harmonize the psychic state, intent on unifying all areas of human life through the principles of harmony. The divine harmony can be grasped through the mind, yet can also be perceived through the senses... through praxis they may be felt in the soul, itself a harmonic entity."*[9]

::

One day as I was contemplating my next move, he appeared and explained to me in simple terms, through words, my purpose.

"You are a teacher."
                    "Me?"
                    "A teacher?"
What exactly would I be teaching? I wondered.

---

[9] Jennifer Gehl, *The Science of Planetary Signatures in Medicine,* page 172.

My mind turned with all of the information I had been consuming. It was hard to keep up some days. My purpose had begun to emerge slowly into my daily life without my knowledge. There wasn't a particular route I felt I must take, but I was sure the more knowledge I acquired the closer I would be to its manifestation.

Although it was now within my power to communicate directly with higher aspects of my soul through the various exercises I had been given, many a time he would receive direct communications with answers to my questions. He was acting as the messenger, providing me with the answers I had sought from my higher consciousness. It was a strange ordeal: me thinking about a question; him, moments later, supplying the answer to a question I had not yet voiced.

::

When we least expect it, the Universe presents us with beautiful opportunities. It was just a normal Saturday morning. I had no reason to question this particular day as anything out of the ordinary, although one day in the future I would come to understand the hidden meaning behind the conversation that unfolded.

During brunch, Jade, my new-found friend from ballet class, announced that she was planning to participate in 'NaNoWriMo'.

"What is that?" I asked with curiosity.

"National Novel Writing Month" she replied. "Starting on 1st November participants work towards a goal of writing 50,000 words, and by the end of the month you will have written a book".

I was positively impressed. "Can I join?" I asked.

"Yes of course," Jade said, "Anyone can take part."

It was open to all who wished to participate and so I signed up that afternoon. It was not a lifelong dream to become a writer - just something I thought may be interesting. I truly loved to read and felt it would be worth a try to see what the other side of creating a book was like. That being said, next to no thought had gone into what I might even write about, but I loved a challenge and the idea of committing to something with a tangible outcome inspired me.

I had a few days before NaNoWriMo was to begin. Suddenly, it occurred to me that I had a story to tell. My love of personal growth, self-awareness, my journey to metaphysics, and views on the age twenty-eight made me feel confident that there was a message to deliver. A few thoughtful hours later and Twenty8 was born. Little did I know I was on the way to discovering my purpose, one word at a time.

With her purpose in one hand, and the golden key in the other; she had reclaimed her power. Her light shined brighter than ever. The fire inside burned with love, passion and meaning. It was her time.

11

Twenty9

As I turned another year older I was tingling on the inside, feeling a sense of power and continued awakening. I was sad this past year was coming to an end but also excited that I was blessed to turn another year older. I hoped I would become another year wiser.

I took it upon myself to conduct a full life review and look at what I was consuming. After everything I had learned from becoming vegan and through all of the teachings from my Magical Metaphysical Man, it felt necessary. I wanted to ensure that the life I was living was as pure as could be, removing as many of the distractions and toxins as possible.

I embarked upon a challenge to undo all of the things that I had been conditioned to do. I may be labelled 'extreme' when I discuss the changes I made next but I believe them only to be 'extreme' considering the current state of the world. They are, in fact, when considering all points of view, the most sensible approach to take if you care about your health and wellbeing.

Health Care

I was approaching my one year anniversary of becoming vegan

when I began to notice that my body was not as vibrant as it had once been. I discovered that there were a number of essential vitamins and minerals that I had not incorporated into my new diet and I was beginning to feel fatigued. As I began to investigate the cause I found that despite all of the beautiful life-foods, there were other nutrients I required. This is a typical pitfall of veganism, and the key is to understand the needs of the body and its nutritional requirements. Just because you are labelled 'vegan' does not necessarily mean you are eating healthily. There are plenty of vegan junk foods and I experimented with them, but found that the more natural my diet was, the better.

I began to research, further understanding the purpose of vitamin c, iodine and minerals. The incorporation of herbal teas and seven planet blends into my diet helped, along with a number of supplements such as sea vegetables, Spirulina, kelp, nutritional yeast, and my favourite item of all, Zell Oxygen. This was what instantaneously perked me up. Zell Oxygen is a complete complex of B Vitamins, enzymes and highly bio-available nutrients. I took this as my Magical Metaphysical Man instructed, combining it in his specially designed morning elixir consisting of 30ml Zell Oxygen in a glass with 1/3 pure water, 1/3 organic beetroot juice, the juice of a whole organic lemon and a pinch of kelp powder.

He explained: *"the Zell Oxygen detoxifies the body, normalises intestinal microorganisms and improves the cytochrome oxidase cellular respiration enzyme chain. When combined with beetroot juice, it increases cell respiration by around 1,000%. The lemon provides vitamins, minerals, and antioxidants. The kelp provides organic iodine and most of the trace minerals of the Periodic Table required for optimal health."*

::

My personal experience with a vegan diet has only been positive. I could never consider returning to my previous eating habits. I have been spoiled with the foods Mother Nature created for us.

This is the most natural, compassionate, healing and healthy way of living. I would fully recommend that you do your own personal research into nutrition so you can be sure you are obtaining all of the correct nutrients.

During my time as a vegan I have managed to maintain a steady body weight, as before I was always slightly underweight. My menstrual cycle is now operating to its own rhythm, like clockwork, whereas before I was forever experiencing painful, long, heavy periods and my cycle was all over the place. Veganism changed so many aspects of my life and I will forever be grateful and an advocate of this lifestyle.

Personal Care

As a newly conscious consumer my entire life was being revamped - this included my personal care regime too. As I read the ingredients list on my shampoo bottle I noticed that not only were some of them not vegan (what animal products were in my shampoo?), but also that I had no idea what the ingredients were. It turns out that most of the constituents were toxins.

According to the Environmental Working Group[10], the average woman uses twelve products containing 168 unique ingredients every day. Men, on the other hand, use six products daily with 85 unique ingredients, on average.

Imagine the unnecessary amount of toxins that are absorbed into the body through these daily personal care regimes. Since I took such great care with my diet then it would only make sense to be discerning about what I was absorbing via my skin, our largest organ.

I transitioned to natural products - not the mass-produced items that just have the rainforest printed on the front to indicate their purity, but rather the actual produce of Mother Nature. My skincare regime consisted of real ingredients which,

---

[10] The Environmental Working Group are a non-profit, non-partisan organization dedicated to protecting human health and the environment. The Environmental Working Group's mission is to empower people to live healthier lives in a healthier environment.

in turn, allowed the body to become even more vibrant, as time was not being wasted removing synthetic toxins.

I turned to Castile soap and oils for face and body. My favourites are jojoba and rosehip oil and I found that coconut oil works wonders as make-up remover. I discovered that apple cider vinegar could be diluted down with distilled water and used as a toner to provide a natural glow to the face.

I took on a challenge of wearing no make-up for thirty days, after which time I realised that the more natural I was, the more authentic I felt in myself. I was going back to basics and it felt so right. It also felt a little rebellious. I was literally sticking two fingers up to the world, as a woman who chose how, why and when to engage in these types of activities. I did not need to wear make-up to feel beautiful. I was beautiful being myself, covering up my face did not make me more attractive and it actually added layers for me to hide behind. Without the make up the mask was gone. The truth of who I was shone through and I felt so confident being comfortable in my own skin.

Considering I was eating a diet high in greens, I required little or no deodorant, opting for a natural substance when needed. Greens play a major part in achieving good body odour and since my diet was so high in these foods I noticed that the concept of deodorant had merely been created to cover up the side effects of our bad diets or hygiene. Medical Daily states: *"eating chlorophyll-rich greens such as spinach and watercress can help freshen up the body, and prevent bad body odour."*

Through my own personal experiments I noticed that as long as I was eating a diet with plenty of fresh greens my body odour was non-existent. However, as soon as I neglected these nutrients I noticed the necessity to use deodorant.

Spiritual Importance of Hair

My experiments with herbs expanded further beyond the use of health-inducing or medicinal teas. I discovered that herbal rinses were very good for the hair, with herbs such as rosemary, yarrow, nettle, chamomile, garden sage, and sagebrush commonly used for this purpose. I experimented with many different herbs to find the perfect blend. There are so many to sample, all of which provide the hair with different nutrients.

This was truly natural hair care, given that the substance I was pouring over my head would have been just as beneficial to drink as a tea - not like the usual goo that comes from a plastic bottle.

After yet another fascinating session with my Magical Metaphysical Man, we covered the topic of the consciousness of hair. This blew my mind. I had always allowed my hair to grow to its fullest length; the longer the better, I felt. But I was unaware that hair served some kind of spiritual importance.

I was surprised to find that hair consists of the most vital sources of energy for a human. According to the yogic tradition, hair is a wonderful gift of nature that helps to raise the spinal Kundalini energy. In India, the "Rishi knot", where the hair is coiled up on the crown of the head during the day, is said to activate the magnetic field or Auric field and stimulates the pineal gland at the centre of the brain.

I then went on to discover how in ancient history hair was cut forcefully, as a symbol of slavery. This was because conquerors understood that the prana would be decreased by doing so, and the slaves would be easier to control. [11]

During the Vietnam War, the Special Forces sought out Native Americans with outstanding, super-natural tracking abilities. A number of the Native Americans enrolled, but were subject to the usual military haircuts. Mysteriously, whatever skills they seemed to possess before, vanished.

When questioned about their failure to perform, they announced that their sixth sense had disappeared and they were unable to tap into their intuition as they had before. The older men were able to identify that this was through the loss of their hair.

The military conducted a test, enlisting another two men, one of whom had his hair cut and the other who was allowed to keep his hair. The results were shocking. Both men had

[11] Source: ultimatetruthofself.com

performed well before the test, but now the one with his hair cut was failing. The one allowed to keep his hair continued to deliver the same, good tracking results[12].

There lies a direct correlation between our hair and our intuition. These stories resonated with me because I had to cut my hair short at one point in my life and I did not feel the same afterwards. It was more than just a change of hairstyle; it was a part of me that had been removed and I somehow felt less powerful. At that point in my life I could not understand why I felt this way, I just knew that I did. It took the best part of three years to grow back. However, based on the stories I have shared, it makes perfect sense. Our hair makes up an important part of our being.

Therefore, we should allow our hair to grow as nature intended. This constant obsession for us to be *perfect* beings free of all bodily hair is absurd. The hair has its purpose and should not be tampered with, or removed through hair removal processes. I personally experimented with what felt right for me and how the removal of any body hair affected my consciousness. I found that certain parts of the body should be left alone. This may sound like 'hippy' living but I feel more centred and comfortable with myself. After all, all you really have to do is ask yourself the question – why do I do this? If it's driven by society, by a need to conform, then resist it. Find what feels good and right for you, not what is expected of you or what society is pitching as the latest trend.

Earth Prana

When was the last time you felt the Earth beneath your feet?

The more inclined I was to live a natural life, one as close to that which Mother Earth intended, the further my studies expanded. I had heard of the concept of 'Earthing' or 'Grounding' before, but never tried it for myself. 'Earthing' is when you are in

---

[12] Source: davidwolfe.com

contact with the Earth's natural, subtle surface electric energy or Ground Prana. There are a number of incredible benefits that can be realised through this simple method of walking on the Earth barefoot.

"Earthing is nothing really new. It's purely a revival of a timeless practice and a forgotten law of Nature: that we belong to Nature, and part of the very connection with Nature is our connection with Mother Earth. "[13]

I challenged myself to thirty days of nature walks, to uncover any difference to my health or wellbeing. After only a few days I was hooked. I remembered putting my shoes back on and walking home from the park only to experience the truly grounding effects of Mother Nature. The Earth's prana, received from the ground into my feet, had sent me off with a tingle, a subtle energetic flow that I had not had before walking barefoot through the park.

After finishing my challenge I never looked back. I noticed an improved mood, relaxed composure and the reduction of headaches (which I typically had through computer usage) - all through Earthing daily. If, for some reason, I had a day off, I was more irritable than usual and I felt less connected to myself.

Illnesses do not come upon us out of the blue. They are developed from small daily sins against Nature. When enough sins have accumulated, illnesses will suddenly appear. – Hippocrates

Electronics

I had little involvement with my television at this point in my journey. I found it of no educational value and therefore the decision was taken to remove it from my home. Luckily, my sister was only too happy to oblige. This space became our music corner, where, should we have time to spare, we would create

---

[13] The Earthing Institute

and learn.

We filled our home with plants - another source of positive life force. Soon after the television was removed, the energy of our home became extremely tranquil and many visitors commented on its peaceful and calming effects.

When encountering the television at other people's homes later I was shocked to see how much advertising was being forced upon us. Most of the advertisements do not even make sense. Whilst reading *No More Secrets, No More Lies* by Patricia Cori, I noted these observations on the subject of advertising:

"Observe in full consciousness the overt messages that appear in advertisements and their actual relationship to the products being sold. Study and record your impressions. How do they make you feel? What is the underlying message? How are you being persuaded or manipulated, and on what levels of consciousness do you respond?"[14]

I was right to question what the underlying message was. I personally did not feel these advertisements had my best interests at heart, nor were they trying to deliver a product that would be valuable to me. Advertisements, almost by definition, are used to manipulate us - manipulate us into feeling less than worthy, playing with our insecurities so we rush out and buy the latest product. I wanted nothing to do with this. There were many times I felt frustrated that those surrounding me did not see nor feel this same manipulation.

Since becoming vegan and a conscious consumer, I had little use for a microwave but it still took up space on my kitchen counter.

After further research into the topic and a session with my nutritionist, this was also removed from my life - especially knowing of the possible emissions of harmful electromagnetic radiation. I also felt that they did not offer nor promote a healthy lifestyle. They encourage the consumption of dead food and this was something that served my living body no purpose.

---

[14] Patricia Cori, *No More Secrets, No More Lies*, page 167.

After dabbling with life without a mobile phone whilst I was away on my travels, I loved the feeling of freedom I found without it. However, after returning home, I began to engage more and more with this device. I found that my zest for life was being sucked out and more often than not I could waste an hour just messing around with it, having achieved nothing.

I was becoming part of the 'zombie smartphone apocalypse' which I hated so. I felt disconnected from the world and the reliance on these devices for everything. Even over dinner, it was impossible for people to go through the whole meal without checking their phones, or worse, answering them.

My Magical Metaphysical Man was particularly scathing when it came to the subject of our ubiquitous mobile phones: *"They are extremely harmful. Just as the tobacco companies suppressed for many decades the fact that smoking causes cancer, so too do the mobile phone companies suppress the truth about the dangers of their products. The standard health and safety tests, which focus on the thermal effects of microwave radiation, are a deception. There are, in fact, many issues of concern unrelated to the heating of brain tissue.*

After just a few minutes' use, a mobile phone alters (and entrains) human brainwaves. The brainwaves will not revert to their normal state for several hours. Since most people are now using their phones throughout the day, their brainwaves will now be almost permanently affected. In a very real sense, the phones are a form of (intentional) mind control. This is why we see people in a state of total addiction.

Not only do phones entrain the user's brainwaves, but they also serve as a source of constant distraction and interruption. The ability to manifest desired events and outcomes, the ability to "create one's own reality" through the power of the mind, requires a process of stable, focused thought; a process of continuous attention. By constantly fragmenting the user's thought-forms and reducing attention span, the endless stream of texts, tweets, social media updates, apps, flashes, and pings from the average mobile phone ensures that the true powers of the human mind are not only disengaged, but also driven to atrophy.

Those today who would wish to maximise the potentials of mind, body and spirit should either discard their phones entirely or, at least, greatly limit their use whilst exploring the available products which purport to minimise their detrimental effects on the physical and subtle-energetic anatomy (such as air-tube headsets, shielding cases and the more esoteric applications of orgonite resins, "Biogeometry" shapes and specific crystals)."[15]

Gratitude

Gratitude had been something that I adopted as a practice many years ago, after I noticed the effects that it had on my life. The art of gratitude made me feel abundant every single day. Whilst everyone else was out there comparing themselves, longing for what they did not have, I was saying thank you for what I did have.

This switch in mind-set automatically moves you into a higher frequency. I saw no need to compare myself to others, as we are all on our own journey. Thus, we are never comparing apples with apples.

My Magical Metaphysical Man provided me with further information on this topic, explaining that, despite the good intentions of many of those teaching about gratitude, the missing key is the *feeling* of gratitude.

For it is the *feeling* of gratitude that changes things and it is important that we understand the energy pattern behind the sentiment.

If you write down ten things you are grateful for every evening before you go to bed but you do not feel the shift in energy as you write then it is an empty exercise. This practice will achieve very little, even if you feel a bit better. In order to create prosperity and encourage more to enter into your life, you must truly feel the value of and an appreciation for every gift and blessing.

---

[15] Esoteric products which claim to harmonise and protect the user's energy or personal living space should always be tested carefully with a pendulum in order to establish whether they expand or contract the wavelength of consciousness.

As my Magical Metaphysical Man explained: *"The energy pattern of gratitude within your consciousness and bio-field will then attract to you by sympathetic resonance more events and gifts about which to feel gratitude. Conversely, if you focus upon the perception of lack, inequality and victimhood (which the mass media perpetually encourage), then you will attract further events which resonate with this energy pattern".*

After discovering this, in the morning, whilst getting ready for the day, I would look around my beautiful home and feel joy and happiness for the roof I had above my head. I would hear my sister clattering around in her room and I would feel happiness and gratitude for her presence in my life. These feelings would continue as I went about my morning. I become so appreciative and grateful that some mornings I would shed a tear for the immense blessings that I had been so lucky to receive into my life.

This is gratitude.

Money & the Importance of Cash

After reading *The Big Money Book* by Robert Lee Camp, I found myself questioning my usual money habits and then changing my ways. I had always owned a credit card, which was used frequently throughout the year, as and when required, perhaps to book a holiday or splurge on a more expensive item that I didn't quite have the cash for immediately. I suspect I was the same as most of us, believing this was normal.

The principles of the book inspired me to dig deep and change my approach to personal finance. My first task was to reduce my spending on unnecessary purchases, so I was able to become debt-free. This was the goal that I held firmly in my mind.

Once I had a better understanding of how credit cards were designed and how they always enticed me to keep coming back for more, I knew I had to break the cycle. I decided to set a monthly spending budget which I took out in cash so that I was not tempted to overspend.

It was a very simple and easy technique to implement, but I found that I began to honour and appreciate my money in a new way.

In the age of contactless payments and card transactions, I feel we can easily bypass the value of money. Tap here, tap there, numbers appear on a screen, transaction done. This is not real. When we withdraw and use cash we can experience the energy transfer in each transaction we complete and we are also able to see, physically, how much money is left in our wallet. This, in turn, helps to create more prosperity and abundance in our lives.

After reading this book and applying these principles to my life, I was able to become debt-free in eight months. I vowed that following my experiences and new found understanding of money I would never use a credit card again. If I wanted something and didn't have the money I would have to wait or go out and find a way to afford it. I felt this approach instantly moved me up a few notches on the prosperity scale. Along with living within my means, which allowed me to budget, I could feel 'financially secure' without gaining any new found wealth, just by adopting better financial principles.

There is much to say on the subject of money but I would highly recommend Robert Lee Camp's book on this subject.

"When we think about just how many years man has been on the planet and how long we have been using paper and plastic to represent money, we can see that it is a very small fraction of the time. Man has always needed ways to store and exchange value and wealth and we have used things such as animals, seashells, and coins made of precious metals. All of these represent value but some of them actually hold intrinsic value. A gold coin, for example, is not just a representation of wealth; it actually is worth whatever is its face value, if not more. Paper money, checks and plastic have no intrinsic value of their own and this puts them in a different category than coins. However, even the coins we use today are fairly worthless. The silver coins have been replaced by copper coated with silver (silver-clad coins) and we really don't even use gold coins as currency.

When we think about getting a message to our subconscious mind of our own value we must consider the way that it interprets and relates to these different forms of currency. What form that we use today would truly represent value to our soul the most?

The soul is relatively slow to adopt new concepts. It takes either repeated affirmations or experiences, or experiences with a highly charged emotional content to set a new pattern in it. In terms of value it's safe to say that our souls just don't recognize the value of credit cards and checks that much." [16]

---

[16] Robert Lee Camp, The Big Money Book, page 38.

Remembering me - an impossible task, after a dramatic year. Thinking back, searching for a clear picture. All I can see now is a blur. A blur of images and thoughts, all so separated from my current being. Remembering me, then. Knowing me, now.

12

Saturn Returns

The more I resonated with twenty-eight as a year of significance the more I came to learn about astrology, something I had little interest in before. This was such a vast subject, and there was much to learn. The more I discussed the topic of my awakening during the year of twenty-eight the more I saw the close correlation with the Saturn Return.

The Saturn Return is when the planet Saturn completes its geocentric orbit to return to the position it held in the zodiac at the time of your birth. This occurs once every twenty-nine years, typically experienced three times during your lifetime, if you are fortunate, around the ages of 28-30, 57-59 and 86-88. The Saturn Return is said to be a time of transformation, a transition from one phase of your life to the next. For me, this truly was a representation of transformation. Each time Saturn Returns we are challenged to discover new levels of awareness.

It was here I discovered that it was not twenty-eight per se but the Saturn Return helping me with my awakening. My mum was right, but she was unaware of the astrological timelines and how they come into play.

Some days I wondered if there was anything my Magical Metaphysical Man did not know.

During one of our lengthy conversations, he requested some of my personal information in order to prepare my natal chart. Thereafter, he would frequently read my chart advising me of key dates, the meanings behind the complex patterns of planetary transits and "directions", and how they would be significant in my life.

In turn, I would ask for a reading whenever I felt I may require the answers from the cosmos. I was captivated by the depth of it all but I knew one day I would have the knowledge to understand how this all worked.

And one day she realised that all of the answers to the secrets of the Universe were there for her to discover. She knew all that needed to be discovered was inside. All she had to do was speak the truth.

13

Inside

After following my intuition and desire for the truth I found that I had a purer heart and my soul was lighter. I was alive with passion, purpose and growing every day beyond my wildest imagination. This truth speaks volumes in the world of fabrication around us. Many people began to take note of my newly found truth and inner peace. They would ask me how I came to be this way.

It was the magic of Twenty8 that brought me here; my age of power. Up until this point, I had never questioned my path, continuing down the same road as everyone else. It was inevitable that I would reach the stage where I began to question life and my true purpose on this planet. Spiritual quests are part of human evolution. Do not be mistaken - you are not alone in your curiosity.

The year I was twenty-eight was the year in which I began to delve into the wonders of veganism, holistic health and metaphysics, something I had never encountered before and something that I never expected would hold such a strong place in my heart. It is something I had not believed I would be so passionate about.

My spiritual evolution took me where I needed to go and I

trust that it will continue to unfold as required. I was blessed with a teacher full of wisdom and knowledge from whom I was able to learn.

Remember the ancient promise of Tibetan Monks: when the student is ready, the teacher will appear.

I have become a whole new version of myself, losing the layers of mistruths, conditioning and expectations. This has allowed me to flourish into the spiritual being I am today. This inner peace occurs when we go inside and do the work required of us, allowing us to achieve this total 'Oneness'. I am not claiming to have achieved this 'enlightenment' however; I am on a path of discovery, which I suspect will fill the rest of my life. It is a lifelong journey I believe and I am only at the bottom of the staircase.

The truth plays a huge part in successfully achieving this inner peace. Without complete and utter honesty we are unable to accept ourselves as we are. This process requires a lot of healing and acceptance, but if you begin where you are today with the truth, the foundation for self-mastery has been laid.

After I found my truth and the unimaginable amount of knowledge there was to learn, I became something of a recluse. I found it incredibly difficult to surround myself with people who were in a deep sleep, so I locked myself up, keeping myself safe in my own little cocoon of love. However, the biggest lesson I learned was that spiritual development was even more important outside my inner world. It is all lovely in the cocoon with no-one there to annoy you or cause stress, but the best way to test your evolution is with those draining things. As time passed I gradually re-established my connection with humanity and I noticed a change.

I began to attract like-minded individuals and share my truth with the world. Not all of them understood it, but then I wasn't meant to be their teacher. I began to live for myself. I found it hard at first but the more I spoke my truth the more it spoke back to me, lifting me with truly beautiful experiences and guiding me closer to my purpose.

Humanity has become so caught up in its web of never-ending lies it is impossible for us to know where to start.

Rather than love, than money, than fame, give me truth.
- Henry David Thoreau

For me, it started with a promise to always speak the truth. The past was gone and now it was time to start anew and cultivate these positive habits. If I didn't really want to attend something, I would immediately reply with a 'thank you, but no thank you' message. I stopped supporting things I didn't believe in and I took my power of choice back.

Instead of my free time being used up on meaningless, thankless tasks I only engaged in activities I truly loved. This left a lot of open space in my diary. As a person who was forever 'busy' before, I found I now had the availability to create and build my dreams. I think we all get easily caught up in this habit of being busy. It's become a 'disease'. A competition, in fact, to find who can have the craziest schedule, who can spend the most hours at the office. It was all thanks to my travels that I learned how to live for the moment, embracing the spontaneity of life through being.

Most importantly, I did not lie to myself anymore. The power that this offered allowed me to move forward with the life I was supposed to be living, the life I had neglected for so long.

The truth was in my soul and now I was speaking it from my heart and through my words. I was in alignment with my inner self and I had embraced my power.

The teachings at the end of this chapter are designed to kick-start your awakening and provide you with some simple principles to revamp all areas of your life.

Summary of Twenty8 Teachings

Many people have asked me how I come to be the way I am today. As you have read from my story, it was not an overnight journey. After turning twenty-nine and when the Saturn Return entered my chart, things began to evolve faster than before. Twenty-eight was only the beginning of my journey.

In the months that followed, while I carefully created this text, a number of truths were uncovered and shared with me. I feel it is my absolute purpose to share this information with you all. I hope you will be inspired by these simple teachings and basic principles for life.

Remember, please take what resonates with you and leave the rest behind.

Love

Love is absolute oneness. Love is the epitome of who we really are. First, we must learn to love ourselves and once this practice is achieved only then we will be ready to engage in a soul connection. Self-love is the foundation for understanding love. Self-love is acceptance of the self, as is. [17]

Truth

Speak your truth. I rarely see humans that are living in line with their truth. Speaking your truth is beyond powerful. When we are honest and live in alignment with the voice inside, everything moves forward and success can be obtained because the soul is at work.

---

[17] Also refer to chapter 1 – Teaching on Love.

Follow your heart

The intelligent mind cannot always understand the interventions of the soul, but it is here that our true purpose can be found. Whatever steals your heart, do that!

Gratitude

Express gratitude for the All That Is. We are extremely blessed to be alive and enjoy the wonders this world can provide us with. Gratitude is a game changer and is something that will change your life if you do it right. Remember you must *feel* the energy flow of gratitude.

Kindness

A little kindness does not go amiss. There are opportunities for us to spread kindness every day. A smile to the stranger in the street, picking up the rubbish that litters the floor of Mother Earth; these are examples of the ways we can be kinder to the world. It is important that we are also kind to ourselves. When we are met with kindness and we operate from this place we can solve a number of problems.

Healing

The secret of healing is in forgiveness. Many of us never heal from our wounds due to the inability to forgive. Forgiveness is not given because we believe the other person is in the right. Forgiveness is given so we can let go, move on and heal. Healing is an extremely important practice. This work must be done so we can be free, light and open.

Freedom of Will

To be free these days seems like some kind of miracle that only the gifted have achieved. It is easy in this world to feel imprisoned. I have experienced this numerous times and I still do not like it. But what we must understand is freedom is a state; it is not a tangible, physical thing. We are always free; we just have to believe we are.

Freedom is available to all. It's whether we decide to remove all of the prison walls we have built for ourselves. Once you do this it will be the most powerful process you ever go through. Nobody owns your power of free will except you.

Spiritual Evolution

Whether we wish to admit it or not, we all have a nagging feeling inside. We all wish to understand our true purpose and bring this forth into fruition. We all have our set journey and we are here to evolve, to learn, to grow, to expand beyond our wildest dreams. Open your mind and expand your frequency. Do not be afraid to seek out your purpose or spiritual evolution. Start with a question, hold this firmly in your mind and be patient as the Universe allows this to unfold.

Breathing

With every breath we take we are breathing in energy. Most of our energy, in fact, comes not from the food we eat but from the air we breathe. Breathing consciously allows one to elevate oneself. This is how 'breatharians' have come to be.

Breatharians are human beings that take their source of energy directly from the air they breathe and therefore no longer require food. This does not mean they starve themselves of essential nutrients; it means they have mastered the art of transforming the universal energy we breathe into the energies which sustain, build and repair the physical body.

Oxygen is our most vital nutrient, needed in order to stay alive. Oxygen is important for two reasons: firstly, the supply of oxygen to our body and organs; and secondly, as it rids the body of waste and toxins.

Yogis understood the importance of the breath and developed various breathing techniques to increase mindfulness and to become aware of living in the present moment, to cure the body of ailments. In yoga, the breath is referred to as prana, meaning energy.

Conscious Eating

Adopt the practice of conscious eating – be fully aware of that which enters your body. The body is the only vehicle we have whilst on Earth. We must treat it with respect and love and fuel it with fresh living foods.

My personal choice is that of a plant-based lifestyle. This brought about my spiritual awakening and allowed me to evolve very quickly thereafter. I have also never been in better health. Do not be fooled by the supermarkets with their pretty packaging. Take the time to check the ingredients list to ensure you are not consuming food that will intoxicate the body and lead to disease.

Sugar, caffeine and alcohol are the main culprits in today's society. They can lead to a whole host of health problems without us even realising how bad they truly are for us.

Be vigilant in your food choices. Eat consciously.

Herbal Medicine

Say goodbye to the pharmaceutical drugs and use herbs. There is no need for us to pop pills on a daily basis when you can use herbs to cure the problem. Nature has the answer to all our problems and it's up to us to start listening to her.

Sun Prana

During my travels, I had never experienced the impact of the Sun in the ways I did while I was living in the Sunshine day after day. This, alongside the solar frequency metaphysics exercise I was taught, led me to believe that the Sun has great meaning and power beyond our understanding.

In ancient Egyptian mythology, the name of the "Sun" god was "Ra", the one who "ra"diates. It is so easy for us to take for granted that which is always there. The Sun shines every day and we rarely stop to appreciate and thank it for its beautiful loving light, warmth and energy.

Although I came to realise the importance of the Sun through my own experiences, I found that other sources backed up my theories.

Trust the Sun. It is a supreme manifestation of All That Is, a fully conscious light being. It is aware of the universal forces of change and resistance; it is assisting in your evolution and Gaia's rebirth.
– Patricia Cori [18]

Earth Prana

The balancing effects of Mother Nature are outstanding. After embarking on an experiment for thirty days, I found that 'Earthing' or 'Grounding' was not only an extremely pleasurable experience but it was also very beneficial to my mood and my mind-set. I could physically feel the effects as soon as my feet touched the soil.

Simplistic Living

My travels allowed me to experience the power of simplicity. Simplistic living contributes to clarity in the mind. When the mind is not cluttered by all of the mess, there is an opportunity for us to live more freely and have more time.

The less we have, the more contentment we are able to feel. I have never found that belongings or things added value to my life. I found that as I stripped away the layers of my life and reverted back to basics, I had more time to concentrate on the good stuff.

I was able to bring about my life's purpose without distraction; I no longer chased material possessions. Life was simple.

We truly need very little to be happy.

---

[18] Patricia Cori, *Atlantis Rising*, page 157.

Music

Be aware and notice how you feel when listening to music. Ensure that you are only allowing positive, healing sounds into your life. Listen to the music of the greats, music that makes you full and alive with energy.

Removal of electronics

Phones, laptops, computers, iPads, Kindles, whatever it is you own make sure you take regular vacations from them. They are sucking the life out of us, making us feel depressed and anxious. It is important that we understand their harmful effects so we can maintain our power.

I would suggest investing in a neutraliser to counteract the waves that are emitted from these electronics. I personally use the Atlantis Radiation Neutralizer which can be purchased from intuitivedowsing.com. It neutralizes or lowers the effect of harmful radiation given off by electrical equipment and it strengthens the auric field against unwanted thought forms.

News

I have not watched, listened to or read the news in over five years. The news is there to scare us and to make us feel fear and devastation. It is strongly manipulated, as well as not really showing us the 'true' news that is occurring in the world. I have never engaged with the news and felt that I am left with a positive upbeat feeling. Ditch it. You don't need it. Those that do watch it will keep you updated, I promise!

My Magical Metaphysical Man had the following to say on this subject: *"There are various groups who wish to control and suppress humanity and they understand the science of manifestation. Via the education system and the mass media, they use the power of your minds, the great power of your focused thought, against you. Millions of people are conditioned to accept extremely limited (and false) ideas about their potentials, whilst inadvertently holding in place the control structures which imprison them through their repeatedly energised fear of war, terror, crime, economic hardship, etc. By turning away from this deliberate mind-programing, you will find that your powers of manifestation greatly increase. So too will you experience a sense of renewed optimism and potential."*

Epilogue

My mission and the purpose of bringing this book to fruition was to present key teachings that will serve to promote healing, joy and the expansion of consciousness and to enable each individual to reclaim their true personal power in alignment with the incarnational purpose of the soul.

I hope though, at the very least, to plant the seeds which will allow your own quest for the truth to unfold.

I hope this book has inspired you to seek out your dreams, overcome hurdles, to be bold in life and love, to live with compassion and in alignment with who you really are.

To be consciously aware is a beautiful gift.

I hope you find your awareness, your answers and your purpose. The world needs it now, more than ever.

Twenty-eight has been the force that will drive the rest of my life. I can't wait to find out what unravels in yours.

Never underestimate yourself or who you can become.

Magical Metaphysical Exercises

Throughout this book I have mentioned various different techniques or exercises given to me by my Magical Metaphysical Man. Some of the exercises and techniques were provided for my specific personal development and are not available for sharing. However, the following may be used for the purposes of healing, protection and rapid spiritual evolution.

This information is free and can be accessed by going to the following link: https://tinyurl.com/twenty8-m-m-e

Interestingly, once I began practising these exercises daily, I encountered a number of energy healers and clairvoyants during social events. In each case (and without me raising the subject), they commented that they could physically "see" (or, in some cases, intuitively sense) that I had a very powerful protective energy field around me, which they were unable to penetrate.

Glossary of Terms

Awakening
Awakening, meaning waking up from the mundane routine of life and understanding our purpose as humans.

Awareness
Noticing your thoughts, actions, words, feelings as often as you can.

Being
Being is to be. To live for the present moment in stillness.

Bio-field
The energetic field or matrix that surrounds the human body.

Carnivore
Meaning meat eater.

Chakra/s
There are seven commonly known chakras inside the body and there are a number of lesser known chakra vortices which are located outside the body.

Chemtrails
Chemtrails (short for "chemical trails") are toxic trails often left by unidentifiable jet aircraft.

Cobalt Mining
The mining of the mineral Cobalt. Cobalt is a key component in rechargeable lithium-ion batteries and is used in smartphones, laptops and electric vehicles. However, there is controversy here because research has uncovered that children as young as 7 are working in these mines.

Conscious
Being aware of your own existence, sensations, thoughts, feelings, surroundings, etc.

Consciousness
The state of being conscious.

Dimension
"Dimension" is not necessarily used as equivalent to spatial dimensions, but more as a frequency band, or level of reality.

Energetic Connection
Upon any connection with another being there will always be an exchange of energy, this energy exchange is the energetic connection.

Energy
A nonphysical force or quality. Everything is made up of energy, even human beings. Energy exists as light, heat, sound, mass, moving objects, gravity, fuel, chemicals, and electricity.

Etheric
Etheric energy is a subtle, primary life energy. The Etheric Body therefore, is another term for the energy body.

HAARP
The High Frequency Active Auroral Research Program (HAARP) was a little-known, yet critically important U.S. military defence project. HAARP is a scientific endeavour aimed at studying the properties and behaviour of the ionosphere, with particular emphasis on being able to understand and use it to enhance

communications and surveillance systems for both civilian and defence purposes. There is a fair bit of controversy around this since it is alleged that the project was designed to forward the US military's stated goal of achieving "Full-spectrum Dominance" by the year 2020 and of "Owning the Weather in 2025".

Higher Dimensional
A higher level above our current dimension where we are in the physical body.

Higher Self
The higher portion of your being or soul that knows all infinite answers.

Higher Source
The 'All That Is', God, the Universe, a source that is received within but is not inherently part of us.

Inner Self
Another term for the Soul, the spiritual part of a person, the part that is not physical, the part of us on the inside that has a strong knowing.

Inner Teacher
Another terminology for the Soul, the spiritual part of a person, the part that is not physical, the part of us on the inside that has a strong knowing.

Life Force
The energy and source of all life.

Metaphysics
The philosophy of understanding existence and knowledge.

Monsanto
Monsanto is an American Agribusiness that is the leading producer of genetically engineered (GE) seed.

Multi-dimensional Identity
All human beings have several dimensions or aspects of their identity.

Plastic Island
An area in the Great Pacific Ocean where plastic rubbish is collecting and causing harm to sea life and the environment.

Prana
The Sanskrit word for "life force".

Purpose
Our individual meaning of life and what we are here to 'do'.

Saturn Return
Saturn Return is when the planet Saturn completes its geocentric orbit to return to the position it held in the zodiac at the time of your birth. This occurs once every twenty-nine years.

Self-containment
The state of being self-contained.

SLS
Sodium Lauryl Sulfate is a widely used and inexpensive chemical that is found in hair care and dental hygiene products which is said to be harmful to our health.

Solar Plexus
The Solar Plexus is located in the back of the navel and is referred to as the third chakra.

Soul
The spiritual part of a person that some people believe continues to exist in some form after their body has died, or the part of a person that is not physical and experiences deep feelings and emotions.

Soul Connection

To connect from a deeper level than that of the physical existence with another being that is a soulmate.

Soulmate

Soulmates may be romantic in nature, others a brother or sister relationship, but ultimately these are people we feel deeply connected to at a higher level. A soulmate may appear for a short period of time to inspire us to grow or remind us who we are, or we may have the pleasure of them being with us for a large part of our journey.

True Self

True Self, meaning who you are on the inside, who you REALLY are on the inside, not what society says or who our parents expect us to be but just who we are organically without trying.

Truth Seeker

A human being who seeks to uncover or find the truth.

Universe

The Universe consists of the whole world including all the planets and galaxies. It is everything that we know and do not know about space.

Vegan

A vegan does not consume meat, dairy products, eggs, honey, or any product derived from an animal.

Bibliography

The following books have shaped and evolved my being and I feel truly blessed to be inspired by these works of art. I believe if you are looking for answers they will help you along your journey to seek the truth.

Atlantis Rising: The Struggle of Darkness and Light by Patricia Cori. North Atlantic Books, 2008, Print.

Health Through God's Pharmacy by Maria Treben. Ennsthaler Gesellschaft GmbH & Co KG, 2004, Print.

Jonathan Livingston Seagull by Richard Bach. Scribner Book Company, electronic version.

LifeFood Recipe Book: Living on Life Force by Jubb & Jubb. North Atlantic Books, 2003, Print.

No More Secrets No More Lies by Patricia Cori. North Atlantic Books, 2008, Print.

Secrets of an Alkaline Body by Jubb & Jubb. North Atlantic Books, 2004, Print.

Sivananda Buried Yoga by Yogi Manmoyanand. O Books, 2008, Print.

Sugar Blues by William Dufty. Time Warner International, 1993, Print.

Taking Charge of your Fertility by Toni Weschler. Vermilion, 2003, Print.

The Big Money Book by Robert Lee Camp. Seven Thunders Publishing, 1997.

The Bridge Across Forever by Richard Bach. A Pan Original, 1994, Print.

The Four Agreements by Don Miguel Ruiz. Amber-Allen Publishing, 1997, Print.

The Power of Now by Eckhart Tolle. Yellow Kite, 2016, Print.

The Science of Planetary Signatures in Medicine by Jennifer T. Gehl. Healing Arts Press, 2017, Print.

The Secret by Rhonda Bryne. Simon & Schuster UK, 2006, Print.

The Secret Life of Plants by Peter Tompkins and Christopher Bird. Harper Perennial, 2002, Print.

Transylvanian Moonrise by Radu Cinamar with Peter Moon. Sky Books, 2009, Print.

Transylvanian Sunrise by Radu Cinamar with Peter Moon. Sky Books, 2011, Print.

Gratitude

My heart bursts at the seams, thinking that just one short year ago I began to keep travel journals which now make up part of the story you have before you. The story of my twenty-eighth year. A tiny thought that maybe I could create a book using these journals has become a reality. In every word there is a thought, a message and an underlying piece of me. I am so grateful to be able to share my story. I have some important people that I must pay my respects and gratitude to - without whom, this book would not have been possible.

To my Mama: Thank you for reading every one of my travel journals while I was away and providing me with the love and motivation to keep writing them. Reading your response emails while I was on my travels and hearing the joy you got from reading them sparked my inner soul to keep creating them. Thank you for always believing in me and knowing I can do anything I set my heart on! Thank you for your philosophy about Twenty8.

To my Sisters: Thank you for your endless hours spent reading my drafts and helping me to shape my story when I was only at the beginning. Thank you for believing in my new path. Thank you both for being an inspiration and chasing your dreams.

To J: Thank you for inspiring me to participate in NaNoWriMo. Without your idea, it is possible that I would have never of started this book. I would also like to thank you for our writing night in November where we mostly talked. The three sentences I got out of that night are some of my favourites!

To Suzie: Thank you for your incredible knowledge and wisdom. Thank you for your time spent answering my many questions! You helped turn my dream into a reality with your fantastic gift of writing. Endless gratitude to you.

To Steve: Thank you for your friendship and saving the day when I was in need.

To Virgil: Thank you for your support and for helping me see that I needed to publish this in my name and own it! Truly grateful for this.

To Paul: Thank you for your honesty when I managed to get all caught up in the process of publishing. Thank you for helping me stay true to myself.

To Jason: Thank you for creating exactly what I wanted. This cover is a direct replication of the vision I had inside but had no idea how to bring into reality. I love it!

Special Acknowledgment

My Magical Metaphysical Man:

Thank you for everything you have gifted me. I hope that the wisdom you shared with me shines out of this book and is clear for all to see.

Words cannot express the immense gratitude, love and admiration that I have for you.

You are always in my mind, my heart and my soul. I will forever be in awe of your honesty, knowledge and wisdom. Thank you for being my guiding light during a time of great change and uncertainty. You are a living embodiment of the truth, the All That Is.

I will be forever indebted to you and only hope the publication of this book somehow repays you, with the knowledge that more will be able to learn from you too.

Twenty8

About the Author

Fabienne is an author, speaker and thought leader. She is the creator of "Fab's Thoughts", where she posts her raw, inspiring, daily thoughts with the world via her popular Instagram feed and website. She can be found either in London, or her 'Magic Island' Ibiza and credits her successes to her attendance at the University of Life.

You can visit her at:

- www.fabsthoughts.com
- https://www.instagram.com/fabsthoughts/